Read Me F

- Descriptions in this manual ar Samsung Galaxy Note 8.
- All information supplied in this guide is for educational purpose only, and users bear the responsibility for using it.
- All information supplied in this guide is what was available as at the time of writing this guide, and it may not be 100% accurate again if there is a major firmware/software update to Samsung Galaxy Note 8.
- Depending on your local network service provider or your location/region, some of the features discussed in this guide may not be available on your Samsung Galaxy Note 8.
- Although I took tremendous effort to ensure that all pieces of information provided in this guide are correct, I will welcome your suggestions if you find out that any information provided in this guide is inadequate or you find a better way of doing some of the actions mentioned in this guide. All correspondences should be sent to pharmibrahimguides@gmail.com

Copyright and Trademarks

Samsung Galaxy Note 8 is a trademark of Samsung, Inc. All other trademarks are the property of their respective owners. Reproduction of this book without the permission of the owner is illegal. Any request for permission should be directed to
pharmibrahimguides@gmail.com.

Copyright © 2017 by Pharm Ibrahim

About This Guide

Finally, a simplified guide on Samsung Galaxy Note 8 is here– this guide is indeed a splendid companion for this high-end phone.

This is a very thorough, no-nonsense guide, useful for both experts and newbies. This guide contains a lot of information on Samsung Galaxy Note 8.

It is full of actionable steps, hints, notes, screenshots and suggestions. This guide is particularly useful for newbies/beginners and seniors; nevertheless, I strongly believe that even the techy guys will find some benefits reading it.

Enjoy yourself as you go through this very comprehensive guide.

PS: Please make sure you do not give the gift of Samsung Galaxy Note 8 without giving this companion guide alongside with it. This guide makes your gift a complete one.

Table of Contents

How to Use This Guide (Please Read!)   ix

Getting Started with Your Phone   1

   Unpacking Your Device   1

   Turning Your Phone on/off and Setting Up Your Phone   3

   Get to Know Your Device   7
      Device Layout   7

   Swiping the Screen Properly   9

   Get to Know Settings Tab   10

   Charging Your Device   12

   Using the Fast Charging Feature   21

   What About the Wireless Charging   23

   Inserting and Managing SD Card/SIM Card   24

   Maintaining the Water and Dust Resistance   44

   Moving Your Items from Your Old Phone to Your Galaxy Note 8   46

   Using the Touch Screen   51

   Using the Dedicated Back Button   53

   Using the In-APP Back Button   54

   Getting to know the Menu icon   55

   Getting to know the Home Screen   56

   Accessing and Managing Applications   82
      Managing the applications screen   86
      Managing Applications   92

   Managing the Navigation Bar   95

   Managing Phone Notifications   97

   Using the Multi Window/Split-Screen Function   101

   Understanding the Quick Settings menu   113

Customizing Your Phone	116
Entering a text	128

Using The Special Features — 134

Using the Fingerprint Feature	134
Iris Scanner	141
Water Resistance	144
The S Pen	144
Removing the S Pen	144
S Pen Layout	146
S Pen and Air View	148
S Pen and Air Command	149
Using the S Pen and the handwriting panel	155
S Pen and Screen Off Memo	156
Changing the tip of your S Pen	157
Using the Always on Feature	158
Live Message	162
Fast Battery Charging	163
Using the Edge Screen on Samsung Galaxy Note 8	164
Using the Edge Panel	165
Using the Edge Lighting	172
Reordering the Edge Screen Panel	175
Managing the Edge Panel Handle Settings/Changing the Edge Panel Location	176
Using People Edge	179
The Bixby	181
Getting started with Bixby	182
Bixby Home	187
Bixby Voice	187
Speaking to Bixby	187
What about Typing?	190
Using Bixby to Open Apps or Programs	192
Using Bixby with Calendar	193
Using Bixby to Set Reminders	194
Using Bixby with Alarm	195
Using Bixby with Clock	196
Using Bixby to Get Flight Information	196
Using Bixby with Weather App	196

Using Bixby with Mail App	197
Using Bixby with Map App	197
What about Math?	198
Using Bixby to Get Definitions	198
Bixby's Settings	198
How to Clear Bixby's Voice Interaction Data	200
Troubleshooting Bixby	201
Conclusion	201
Bixby Vision	202

Using the Web — 204

Internet App — 204
Opening the Internet Browser	204
Get to Know the Internet Browser Interface	204
Customizing the Home Page	207
Using the Address/Search Bar	209
Zooming a Webpage in Internet Browser	210
Using Tabs on Internet Browser	211
Favorites (Bookmarks)	214
Accessing Your Bookmarks/Favorites	216
Saving a Webpage	216
Accessing Your Saved Pages	217
Changing the Search Engine	218
Making Internet App Your Default Browser	218
Managing the History List	219
Sharing a Webpage with Friends	220
Add Your Favorite Webpage to the Home Screen	220
Printing Web Pages on the Internet browser	221
More on Internet browser Settings	223
More on the Menu Icon	223
Troubleshooting the Internet browser	224
Troubleshooting Internet Connection when Using the Internet Browser	225

Communication — 227

Calling — 227
Making, Answering, Rejecting and Silencing a Call	227
Learn How to Use Your Phone During a Call	232
Emergency Calling	235
Using Call Waiting	236
Using the Speed Dial Options	236
Using the Fixed Dialing Option	238
Call Forwarding (Diverting Calls to Another Number)	239

Block Calls	241
What about Caller ID	242
Using the Messaging app	243
EMAIL APP	249
Introduction	249
How to Add Your Email Accounts to the Email app	249
Special Note on Adding Exchange Account to the Email App	250
How to Compose and Send an Email Message Using the Email App	250
Attaching a file	254
Managing a Received Email	255
How to Open and Save an Attachment in the Email App	257
Managing the Settings Options	258
How to Remove the Default Email Signature in the Email App	260

Personal Information — 262

Contacts	262

Accessibility Features – the Special Features for Easy Usage — 274

Vision	274
Hearing	275
Dexterity and Interaction	276
More settings	277
Services	278

TOOLS — 279

Easy Mode	279
Do Not Disturb	281
Creating Schedules and More with the Calendar App	284
Using the Camera	288
Recording a video	293

Connectivity — 295

PC Connections	295
Wi-Fi	298

Using Your Phone as a Hotspot — 300

Access More by Using Bluetooth — 302

Location Services — 304

Find My Mobile Feature — 305

Using the NFC (Near Field Communication) — 310

Settings — 312

What You Must Know About Samsung Galaxy Note 8 — 314

How to Find Your Phone When lost — 314

How to Reduce Your Mobile Data Usage on Samsung Galaxy Note 8 — 314

Solution to Non-Responding Apps — 316

How to Conserve Samsung Galaxy Note 8's Battery Life — 317

What to Do if You Forget You Device Lock Screen Password/Pin — 319

How to Take Screenshot on Your Device — 323

The Smart capture — 324

Extras — 326

What You Must Know Before Selling or Giving Away Your Samsung Galaxy Note 8 — 326

Getting an antivirus for your phone -- is it necessary? — 327

Safety Precautions When Using Samsung Galaxy Note 8 on Wi-Fi — 328

I am Having a Dwindling Love for my Samsung Galaxy Note 8; What Should I Do? — 329

TROUBLESHOOTING — 331

Safety precautions — 334

Just Before You Go (Please Read!) — 336

How to Use This Guide (Please Read!)

This guide is an unofficial manual of Samsung Galaxy Note 8 and it should be used just like you use any reference book or manual.

To quickly find a topic, please use the table of contents. This will allow you to quickly find information and save time.

When I say you should carry out a set of tasks, for example, when I say you should tap **Settings >Sound> Notifications & actions**, what I mean is that you should tap on **Settings** and then tap on **Sound**. And lastly, you should tap on **Notifications & actions**.

I hope this guide helps you get the most out of your smartphone.

Getting Started with Your Phone

Unpacking Your Device

It is quite easy to unbox you Samsung Galaxy Note 8. Just use your hand to press the inner box so that it sticks out. Then use a knife to cut the seal (if any) and carefully open the box.

When you unpack your product box, check your product box for the following items:

1. Samsung Galaxy Note 8 with S Pen
2. USB charging cable & power adapter
3. Quick Start Guide
4. Earphones
5. Tweezers and Pen nibs
6. USB connector (USB Type-C)
7. Eject Pin (the eject pin is located on the case that house the "quick start guide")
8. Micro USB Connector

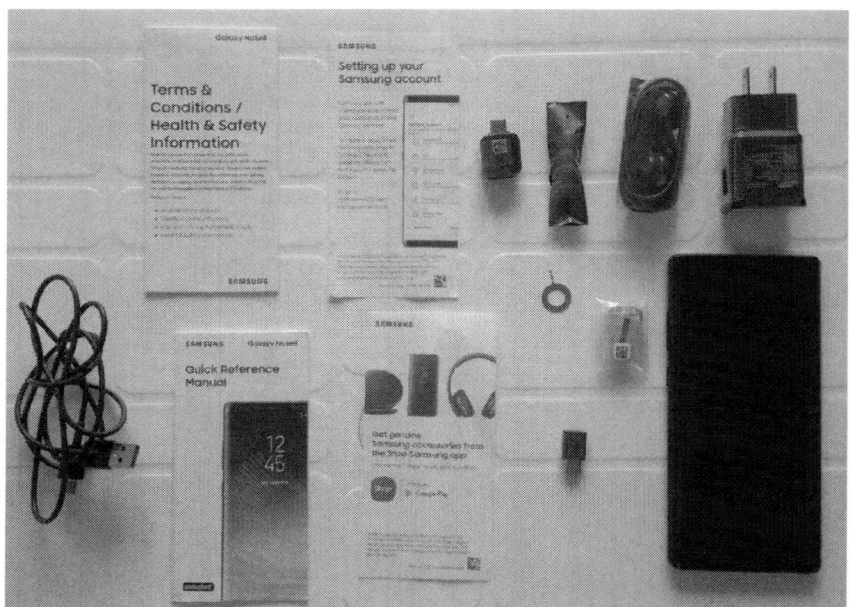

Hint: I will advise that you are careful when removing the eject pin from the case (the eject pin is located on the case that houses the "quick start guide") so as not to prick your hand in the process.

Turning Your Phone on/off and Setting Up Your Phone

Just like many other smartphones, turning on your device is as simple as ABC. To turn on your phone, press and hold the Power Key until you notice a small vibration. If you are turning on your phone for the first time, please carefully follow the on-screen instructions to set it up. You will have the option to connect to a Wireless network during the setup, to learn more about connecting your phone to Wi-Fi, please go to page 298. In addition, I will advise that you insert the SIM Card before switching on your phone. To learn more about inserting the SIM card, please go to page 24.

To turn off your phone, press and hold the power key and select **Power off.** Select **Power Off** again to confirm.

I addition, if you are using your phone for the first time, remove any protective nylon from the surface of the phone.

Please do not vex if you find it unnecessary reading about how to on/off your device. I have included it, in case there may be someone reading this guide who is a complete novice and knows close to nothing about smartphones.

Tips:

- Some network provider may require you to enter a PIN when you switch on your phone. You can try entering **0000.** This is the default PIN for many network providers. If you have problem entering the correct PIN, please contact your network service provider.
- During the setup, you may skip a process by tapping **SKIP** located at the bottom of the screen. Usually, you will have the option to perform this process in the future by going to your phone settings.
- While using your phone for the first time, you may have the option to transfer your contents from your old phone to Samsung Galaxy Note 8. Just carefully follow the onscreen instructions to do this. If you skip the process of content transfer during the phone setup, and you will like to perform the transfer now, please see page 46 to learn how to go about this.
- Because of software updates, it is likely that your phone will consume a large amount of data during the setup, I will advise that you connect to a wireless network if you can. Using a mobile network during the setup may be expensive.
- When you start using your phone, you may probably notice that your phone screen locks within few seconds after you

finish interacting with it. To allow your phone stay longer before it locks, change the screen timeout setting. To do this:
- Swipe down from the top of the screen and select Settings icon ⚙.
- Tap **Display**.
- Scroll down and tap on **Screen Timeout**. Then choose an option.

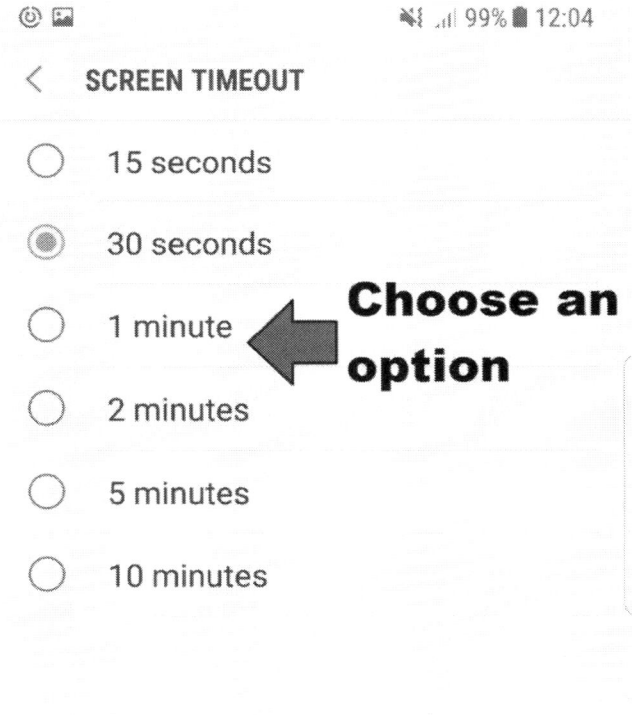

Please note that selecting a longer timeout may make your battery discharge faster.

- *Do you need to charge your phone before first use?*

To the best of my knowledge, it is not necessary. If you charge it before first use, that is cool but if there is no way to charge it, then you can use it straightaway without charging it. I have learnt that the new lithium batteries used in smartphones don't really need to be charged before first use (provided that the battery still has power).

Get to Know Your Device

Device Layout

Number	Function
1.	LED indicator. This gives different colors depending on what is happening on the phone.
2.	Iris Detection LED

7

3.	Proximity sensors
4.	Receiver/Earpiece
5.	Front camera
6.	Iris Scanner
7.	Power button
8.	Touch Screen
9.	Bixby button
10.	Volume up and down button
11.	Rear camera
12.	Rear camera
13.	Flash
14.	Fingerprint Sensor
15.	Heart Rate sensor
16.	S Pen
17.	Headset jack
18.	USB port and charging port (multipurpose port)
19.	Microphone. Please ensure you don't block the microphone while making a call.
20.	Speaker
21.	S Pen/S Pen port
22.	SIM and Memory Card Tray

Swiping the Screen Properly

From time to time, you will need to interact with the screen of your phone by swiping it with your finger. If you don't swipe it properly, you may not get the expected result. You can swipe to perform the following actions:

1. **Access the notification menu/quick settings**

To access the notification menu/quick settings, swipe from the top of the screen. Please make sure you are starting from the top of the screen (around the earpiece/receiver area) to get the expected result. See the picture below.

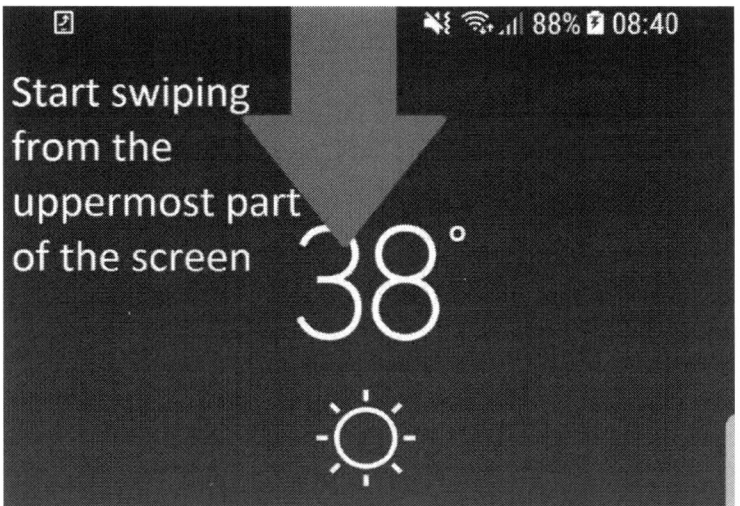

2. **Accessing the app screen**

To access the applications screen, swipe up from the lower part of the screen. See the direction of the arrow below.

Tip: To go back while on the applications screen, just swipe up or down from the middle (or around the middle) of the screen.

Get to Know Settings Tab

I am talking about settings tab under this section because I will be referring to this tab a lot.

The settings tab has many subsections and because of this, I will advise that you use the Search menu (denoted by the lens icon) to quickly find what you are looking for. To use the setting's search feature, swipe down from the top of the screen and tap the settings icon (see the picture below).

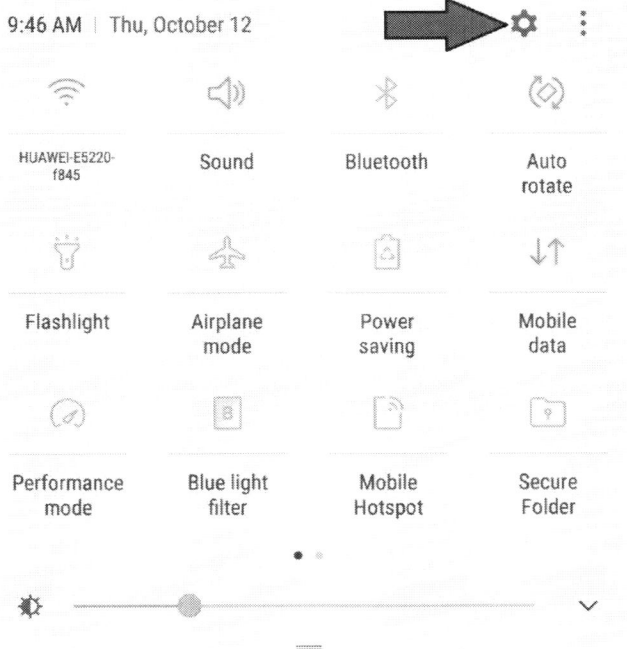

Then tap on the search icon and type a keyword corresponding to the settings you are looking for. For example, if you are looking for settings relating to battery, just type **Battery** into the search bar. The result filters as you type.

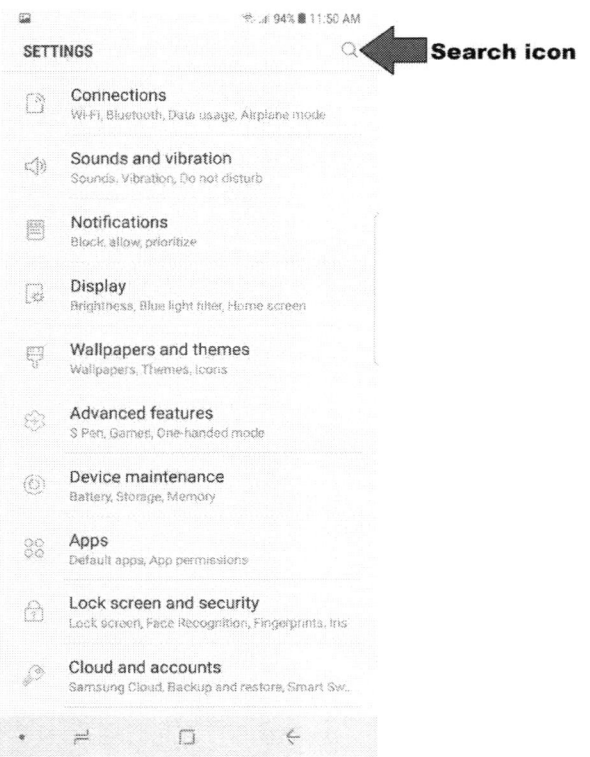

Charging Your Device

If you are using your Samsung Galaxy Note 8 more often (especially if you use Wi-Fi more frequently), you may realize that you need to charge your phone every day. One of the coolest times to charge your device is when you are taking a shower, as you are not likely to be using it at the time.

Do you need to charge your phone before the first use?

12

To the best of my knowledge, it is not necessary. If you charge it before the first use, that is cool. But if there is no way to charge it, then you can use it straightaway without charging it. I have learnt that the new lithium batteries used in smartphones don't really need to be charged before the first use.

To learn more on how to use your phone for a longer time on battery, please go to page 317.

To charge your Samsung Galaxy Note 8:
1. When you first open your product box, you will notice that the power cord consists of two parts (i.e. the USB cable and the USB power adapter), connect these two parts together. See the picture below.

2. Connect the end of the USB cable to the charging port of your device, making sure that both the charging cable and the charging port on your device make a good and firm contact.

3. Plug the power adapter to an electrical outlet. When your phone is charging, a charging icon will appear at the top of the screen. When your phone is fully charged, the battery icon will appear solid/full.

Note: After charging, you may need to apply a small force to remove the USB cord from the phone. Please be careful so that the phone does not mistakenly drop from your hand in the process.

4. To know the remaining charging time, swipe down from the top of the screen and then tap **Settings** ⚙ > **Device Maintenance** > **Battery**. The charging time may be longer if you are using your device while charging it.

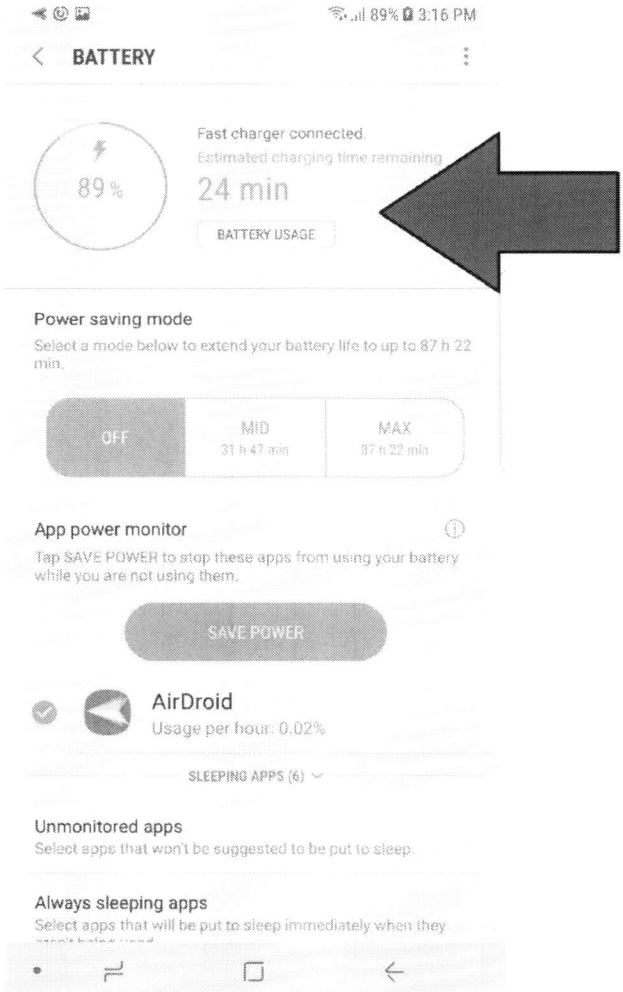

Tips:

- To extend the power of your device substantially, swipe down from the top of the screen and then tap **Settings** ⚙ > **Device Maintenance** > **Battery**. Under **Power saving mode** tab, tap MID or MAX and then tap **APPLY...**

 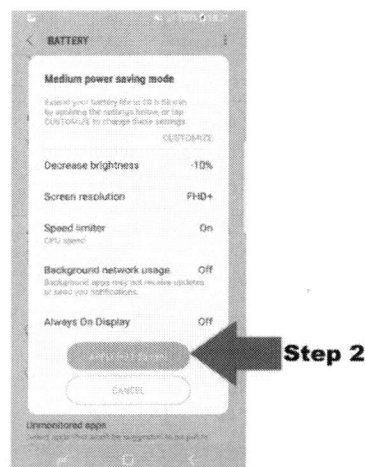

- There are some apps out there that will consume your battery even without using them. Interestingly, you can prevent these apps from this behavior. To do this, swipe down from the top of the screen and then tap **Settings** ⚙ > **Device Maintenance** > **Battery**. Under **App power monitor** tab, select the apps you want to prevent and tap **SAVE POWER**.

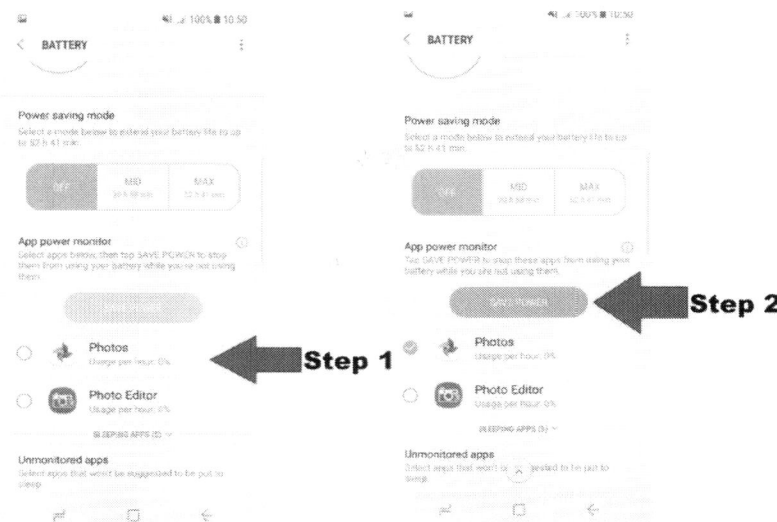

In addition, if there is an app that you want to give unrestricted battery access to, tap **Unmonitored apps** (located at the bottom of the screen) and then tap **Add apps**. Select the app you want and tap **DONE** located at the top of the screen.

17

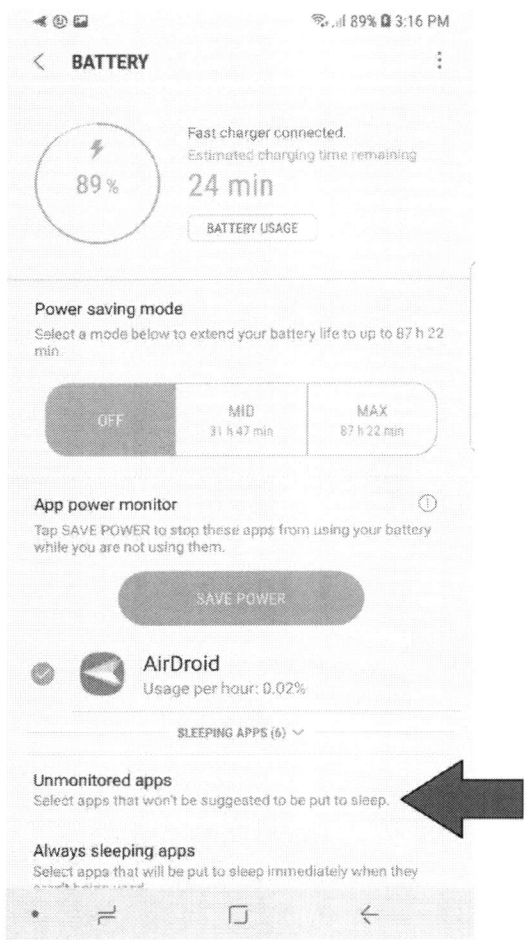

Tip: To remove an app from **Unmonitored apps** tab, tap **Unmonitored apps** and tap the menu icon. Select **Delete apps** and choose the app(s) you want to delete. Tap **Delete** to remove the app from Unmonitored apps tab. Note that the app is not removed from your device, it is only removed from those apps that have unrestricted access to your battery.

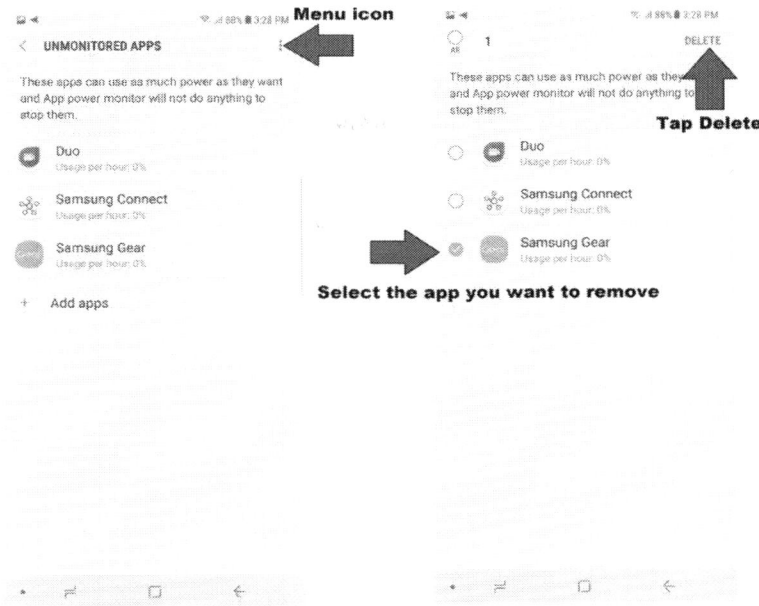

In addition, if you don't want an app to be consuming your battery you can put it to sleep. To do this, just go to the app screen, tap and hold the app you want to put to sleep and select **Sleep**. To wake up a sleeping app, just launch the app.

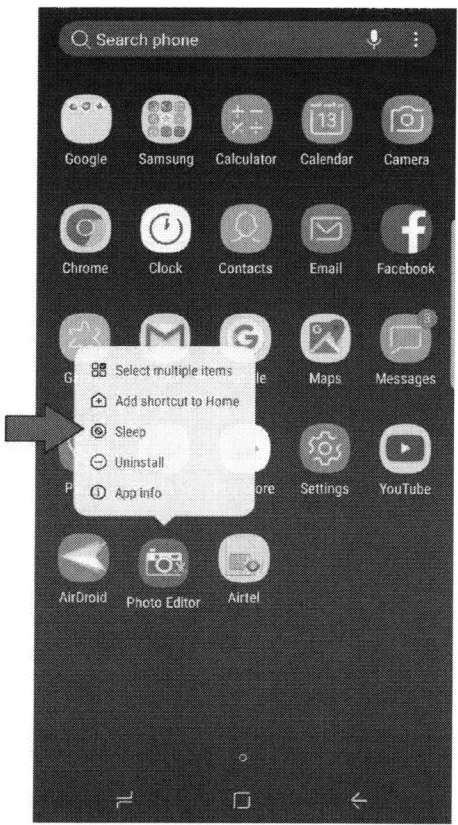

Please note that not all app can be put to sleep.

Note: Please note that it is not advisable to use the multipurpose port while it is wet. If your phone has contact with water or any watery substance, please make sure you dry the multipurpose port before using it. Although your device is water resistant, it is not advisable at all to charge it while the device is wet. This may cause an electric shock or damage your device.

Multipurpose jack

Using the Fast Charging Feature

Your device is built with a battery charging technology that charges the battery faster by increasing the charging power. This feature can allow you to charge your Samsung Galaxy Note 8 up to 50% in about 40-50 minutes.

Please note that using your phone while charging may affect the time your phone is going to take to make a complete charging cycle.

Tip: You can enable or disable the fast charging settings by going to Settings > **Device Maintenance** > **Battery**. Then tap on menu icon located at the top of the screen. Select **Advanced Settings** > **Fast cable charging**.

Furthermore, you may not be able to use the fast charging feature when you charge the battery using a standard battery charger. To use **Fast Charging** on your device, you will need to connect it to a battery charger that supports Adaptive fast charging like the one that came with your device. To know if a battery charger supports this feature, check the charger.

Although the fast charging technology on Samsung Galaxy Note 8 is a cool feature, it may still be affected by factors like the temperature of the phone. If the device heats up for one reason or the other, the charging speed may decrease.

What About the Wireless Charging

Samsung Galaxy Note 8 has a built-in wireless charging feature and this means that you can charge the battery on your device using a wireless charger (sold separately).

To charge your device wirelessly:

- Using a USB cord, connect the power adapter that came with your device to the wireless charger (sold separately) and then plug it to a wall socket. Please note that if you are using a wireless charger that is not made by Samsung, your power adapter may not work with your wireless charger. If this is your situation, then buy a separate power adapter for wireless charge.
- If you are using your wireless charger for the first time, remove any protective nylon from the surface of the wireless charger. Then place your mobile device on the wireless charger following the instructions provided by the manufacturer of the wireless charger. Please note that if you connect a charger to your mobile device during wireless charging, the wireless charging feature may be unavailable.

In addition, depending on the type of the wireless charger you are using, charging wirelessly may take a longer time when compared to using a cable. This means that if you want to charge your device faster, you may consider using a cable.

Inserting and Managing SD Card/SIM Card

Samsung Galaxy Note 8 supports the use of external memory card.
To insert memory card or SIM Card:
1. Locate the SIM and SD Card tray on the top edge of the device and gently insert the eject tool included with your

phone into the eject hole (located at the top edge of your phone) and then push until the tray pops out. *Please note that you may need to apply small force before the tray pops out.*

2. Pull out the tray gently from the tray slot and place the SIM Card on its tray and the SD Card on its tray. Make sure the metallic contacts on the SIM and the SD Card are facing down.

Hints: *Please note that SIM 2 may not be available on your phone if you don't buy the dual SIM version. In addition, if you are using the dual SIM version, you may not be able to use a second SIM and the external memory card at the same time. This is because both the second SIM (SIM 2) and the external memory card use the same space.*
*However, you may still be able to get a second SIM and external memory card to work simultaneously if you use a dual SIM adapter. Just search for **dual SIM adapter** on amazon.com to get started.*
After inserting the SIM(s), the whole setup will look like this. See the picture below.

3. Slide the card tray back into the slot.
4. Please note that if the SIM Card or the memory card is not inserted properly, your phone may not recognize it. Please endeavor to follow the instructions above to avoid this.
5. To locate the memory card after inserting it, swipe up from the bottom of the screen, and tap **Samsung folder > My Files**, and then tap the **SD Card** folder.

Note: Since your device is water resistant, you may be tempted to drop it in water at one time or the other, please make sure that you fully insert the card tray into the tray slot to prevent liquid from entering your device.

As a rule, you must always make sure you prevent water from entering the inner compartment of the phone. Therefore, please make sure you properly close any slot you have opened on your phone before inserting it into water. However, S Pen slot does not need to be closed before inserting your phone into water.

Hint: When the memory card is properly installed you should see the memory card icon on the status bar at the top of the screen.

To remove the SD Card:
1. Swipe down from the top of the screen and select the settings icon ⚙ .
2. Tap **Device Maintenance**

```
                         ▼  .ıl 64%  06:39
 SETTINGS                                    Q

          Wallpapers and themes
          Wallpapers, Themes, Icons

          Advanced features
          Games, One-handed mode

          Device maintenance          ⬅
          Battery, Storage, Memory

          Apps
          Default apps, App permissions

          Lock screen and security
          Lock screen, Face Recognition, Fingerprints...

          Cloud and accounts
          Samsung Cloud, Backup and restore, Smart...

          Google
          Google settings

          Accessibility
          Vision, Hearing, Dexterity and interaction

          General management
          Language and input, Date and time, Reset
```

3. Tap **Storage.**

DEVICE MAINTENANCE

99 /100

EXCELLENT!

Your phone's maintenance status is excellent.
Tap below to improve it.

Battery	Performance mode	Storage	Memory	Device security
Charging...	Optimized	52.1 GB free	1.4 GB free	Deactivated

4. Tap the **menu icon** (the three dots icon located at the top of the screen).

5. Tap **Storage settings**
6. Tap **Unmount icon** and gently open the SD Card slot using the ejection pin (as you have done above). Close the SD Card slot when you are done removing the memory card.

STORAGE

DEVICE STORAGE

11.90 GB
Used out of 64.00 GB

Internal storage
11.90 GB used of 64.00 GB

PORTABLE STORAGE

SD card
94.69 MB used of 31.24 GB

Unmount icon ←

Please note that if you unmount the memory card without removing it from your device, you will need to mount it before it can be accessed again. To mount your memory card, follow the steps one to five above and then tap **Unmounted** and then select **Mount** when prompted.

Encrypt SD Card

You may wish to encrypt your memory card for extra security.

- From the Home screen, swipe up from the bottom of the screen and tap **Settings.**
- Tap **Lock screen and security**
- Scroll down and tap **Encrypt SD card.**

LOCK SCREEN AND SECURITY

SECURITY

Samsung Pass
Verify your identity with biometrics instead of a username and password.

Find My Mobile
Locate and control your phone remotely if it's lost or if you forget your unlock method.

Unknown sources
Allow the installation of apps from sources other than Play Store or Galaxy Apps.

Secure Folder
Keep your personal files and apps safe and secure.

App permission monitor
On

Secure startup
Protect your device by using a screen lock when your device turns on.

Encrypt SD card
Protect your SD card by encrypting its data.

Other security settings
Change other security settings, such as those for security updates and credential storage.

- Please read all the onscreen information that appears.

> ◻ ▪   📶 82% 🔋 6:02 PM
>
> < **ENCRYPT SD CARD**
>
> ┌───┐
> │ You can encrypt SD cards. Encrypted SD cards │
> │ can only be read on the device used to encrypt │
> │ them. Tap ENCRYPT SD CARD to start the │
> │ encryption process. │
> │ │
> │ Encryption could take an hour or more. Before │
> │ you start, make sure that the battery is charged │
> │ and keep the device plugged in until encryption │
> │ is complete. During the encryption process, the │
> │ SD card cannot be used. If your device is reset to │
> │ factory default settings, it will be unable to read │
> │ encrypted SD cards. │
> └───┘
>
>   ⬆
>
>   **Read all the information above**

- If you are satisfied with the information, then tap **Encrypt SD card** located at the bottom of the screen and follow the onscreen instructions to encrypt all data on your memory card.

When you encrypt your memory card, you may need a numeric PIN or password to decrypt your SD card when you first access it after switching on your device. In addition, *please note that encrypting a memory card may make it unreadable on another device.*

Formatting the memory card

1. Swipe down from the top of the screen and select the settings icon ⚙ .
2. Tap **Device Maintenance**

3. Tap **Storage.**

4. Tap the **menu icon** (the three dots icon located at the top of the screen).

5. Then select **Storage settings**
6. Tap **SD card**. (Please make sure you are tapping SD card and not the unmount icon next to it).

7. Tap **Format**, read the onscreen information and then tap **Format**.

Please note that formatting a memory card will cause you to lose all the files stored on the memory card and you may need to backup your files before initiating this process.

To transfer apps from internal storage to SD Card:

1. Swipe down from the top of the screen and tap **Settings** ⚙.
2. Tap **Apps**.
3. Tap the app you want to transfer.
4. Select **Storage** from the options that appear.
5. Next to the name of the app you want to transfer, tap **Change**.

Please note that this option may not be available for all apps. In fact, I have noticed that the "change" option is not available for most of apps that came with the phone.

6. Tap **SD card**.
7. Tap **Move** located at bottom of the screen and wait for the process to complete.

Tip: You may consider removing temporary files from your device to free up space. From the Home screen, swipe up from the bottom of the screen and tap **Settings** > **Device Maintenance**. Tap **Storage** and tap **Clean Now**.

Please note that using this method may clear cached data for all apps.

Tip: If your phone is hanging or misbehaving, consider cleaning the memory. To do this, from the Home screen, swipe up from the bottom of the screen and tap **Settings** ⚙ > **Device Maintenance**. Tap **Memory** and tap **Clean Now**.

☼ ▶ 🖼 ...   🔇 📶 83% 🔋 08:13

< **MEMORY**

2.2 GB
/4 GB

System and apps: 2.2 GB
Available space: 1.1 GB
Reserved: 672 MB

To improve performance, free up memory by stopping background apps.

➡ CLEAN NOW (+699 MB)

✓ ▶ **Google Play Store**
Memory : 128 MB, CPU : 0.00%

✓ 🅱 **Hello Bixby**
Memory : 33.3 MB, CPU : 0.00%

✓ ❁ **Gallery**
Memory : 38.4 MB, CPU : 0.00%

VIEW MORE ⌄

Maintaining the Water and Dust Resistance

Although your Samsung Galaxy Note 8 and the S Pen are water and dust resistant, there are few things you still have to put at the back of your mind so that you don't spoil your phone/S Pen. Some of the things you have to know are discussed below:

- Even though your device is water resistant, you can't still immerse the device in water deeper than 1.5 m and/or keep it submerged for more than 30 minutes.
- The screen of your device may not respond properly while under water or wet. I will advice that you clean it with a dry towel to get the full functionality. However, you can write notes with the S Pen while the phone is submerged under water.
- It is not advisable to put your device under water moving with force such as tap water. This is because water may get into the inner part of your device in the process.
- While your screen is wet, you may not enjoy the optimal function of your device as you should. You may need to clean it with a dry towel to make it work properly.
- To avoid electric shock, please don't charge your device while it is wet or while it is under water.
- Avoid putting your phone in a liquid other than water.

Hint: In my test, I found out that Samsung Galaxy Note 8 doesn't respond to touch while under water but responds to touch immediately you take it out of water. You don't even need to clean/dry it before you start using it. But don't forget that you can't drop it inside water while the SIM/memory slot is opened. In addition, please don't charge your phone while it is wet to avoid electric shock.

Moving Your Items from Your Old Phone to Your Galaxy Note 8

You can move your files to your new phone by following one of the steps mentioned below:

- The easiest way to transfer your items from your old phone (Android Phone or IOS Phone) to your new Samsung Galaxy Note 8 is through the use of USB connector (On-the-Go (OTG) connector) and a USB cable. To use this method, please follow the instructions below:

Please make sure you download and install Smart Switch app on your old phone before you begin the transfer process. Smart Switch can be downloaded from Google Play Store. In addition, this method of data transfer consumes large amount of energy, make sure your phone is fully charged before initiating this process.

  - Plug the USB connector (On-the-Go (OTG) connector) that came with your device into the multipurpose jack of your device.

  OTG Connector

  - Then connect your device and the old phone using a USB cable. Please note that you should select Media device (MTP) option on your old phone if prompted. The whole connection will look like this.

- When prompted, tap **Smart Switch** and then tap **START**. If you are not prompted, disconnect the cable, then reconnect. Your device will recognize the old phone and a list of data you can transfer will appear.
- Follow the on-screen instructions to transfer data from the old phone.
- Alternatively, if the USB connector and the USB cable are not accessible, you can send items from your old phone to your new phone wirelessly using Smart Switch app. Please note that you will need to download and install **Smart Switch** on your Old phone to complete this process. Smart Switch can be downloaded from Google Play Store.

47

- On your device, swipe down from the top of the screen and tap Settings icon ⚙, tap **Clouds and Accounts** and then tap **Smart Switch**.
- Open the **Smart Switch** app on your old phone.
- Tap **Start** and tap **Agree**.
- Tap **Wireless** and then tap **Receive**.

- On your Samsung Note 8 device, select the operating system of the old phone from the list.
- Follow similar steps on your old phone. You may need to download and install Smart Switch on your old phone if you don't already have it. If you are using Android, Smart Switch can be downloaded from Play Store. In addition, you will select **Send** on your old phone (don't forget that you selected **Receive** on your new phone).

- Follow the on-screen instructions on both your new phone and the old phone to complete the transfer process.
- When the transfer process is complete, tap **Close App**.
- I will like to mention that you can also transfer items from your old phone to your new device using memory card. All you have to do is to insert a memory card into your old phone, copy your items on it, remove the memory card and then place it inside your Samsung Galaxy Note 8.
- Lastly, you can transfer your items from your old phone to your new phone by using cloud storage. For example, you can use OneDrive App. To do this, add files to OneDrive app on your old phone so that you can access them from your Samsung Galaxy Note 8. To move a file to OneDrive, just drag and drop the files to your OneDrive folder. The files will be uploaded to OneDrive when you have an internet connection on that device.

Once the files are on your OneDrive, you can access them on your Samsung Galaxy Note 8 by opening OneDrive app. To avoid any problem while trying to access your files, please ensure that you are connected to a network while trying to access OneDrive.

Please note that you may need to download OneDrive app to your phones to use this last method.

Using the Touch Screen

Your phone's touch screen allows you to easily select items and perform functions. With the touch screen, you may operate your phone like a pro.

Notes:

- Do not press the touch screen with your fingertips, or use sharp tools on the touch screen. Doing so may cause malfunctioning.
- Do not allow the touch screen to come into contact with other electrical appliances. This may cause the touch screen to malfunction.
- When the touch screen is wet, endeavor to clean it with a dry towel before using it. The touchscreen may not function properly when wet.
- For optimal use of the screen, you may need to remove screen protector before using it. However, a good screen protector should be usable with your phone.

You may control your touch screen with the following actions:
Tap: Touch once with your finger to select or launch a menu, application or option.
Tap and hold: Tap an item and hold it for more than a second to open a list of options.

Tap and drag: Tap and drag with your finger, to move an item to a different location in the application grid/list.

Pinch: Place two fingers far apart, and then draw them closer together.

> **To Lock or Unlock the touch screen**

When you do not use the device for a specified period, your device turns off the touch screen and automatically locks the touch screen so as to prevent any unwanted device operations and also save battery. To manually lock the touch screen, press the power key. To unlock, turn on the screen by pressing the power key (or double tap the home button ▢) and then swipe in any direction. If you have already set a lock screen password, you will be prompted to enter the password instead of swiping.

Note: You can change the lock screen method on your phone, please refer to page 127.

Rotating the touch screen

You phone has a built-in motion sensor that detects its orientation. If you rotate the device, the interface will automatically rotate according to the orientation.

> **To activate or deactivate screen rotation**

To quickly disable or enable screen rotation, swipe down from the top of the screen and tap ⟳.

Using the Dedicated Back Button

You may use the dedicated back button (see the picture below) to view the previous page or go back to a previous menu. Back button can also be used to close a dialog box, menu, or keyboard.

In addition, you may use the dedicated back button on your device to get out of any page when you are done with the page and you don't see the done option.

Using the In-APP Back Button

There are some apps that give you the opportunity to go back to a previous screen using the in-app back button ⟨. When available, this button can be found at the upper left part of the screen.

In-App Back Button

⟨ ACCESSIBILITY	🔍

CATEGORIES

Vision

Hearing

Dexterity and interaction

MORE SETTINGS

Text-to-speech

Getting to know the Menu icon

The menu icon is the three dots icon that usually appears at the top of the screen when you open an app. This icon can also be called **hidden options icon**. This is because it contains more options about an app or item.

Hint: Whenever you are thinking of accessing more options when using an app/item, just tap on the menu icon.

Getting to know the Home Screen

From your home screen, you can view your phone's status and access applications. Scroll left or right to see different apps on the home screen. Please note that the home screen usually has many screens and you can add more screens to the home screen by tapping on +

Home Screen Layout:

Number	Function
1.	Notification icon/ Status icons
2.	Weather widget. This widget may not be visible if

	you have not allowed it, to make weather widget visible, while on Home screen, tap and hold the screen and select **Widgets.** Swipe the screen until you see **Weather,** and tap it. Then tap and hold **Weather** widget and move it to the desired home screen.
3.	**Edge Handle**: Swipe left on this handle to display edge icons.
4.	**Home Screen Indicator:** This indicates which home screen is currently visible
5.	**Back Button**.
6.	**Home Button**
7.	**Recent App button**
8.	**App shortcuts**: Launches your favorite application
9.	Notification icon/ Status icons

Managing the Home Screen

To get more out of the home screen, you will need to perform some tweaks. To customize the home screen to your taste:

- While on the home screen, place your two fingers on the screen and then move them closer, or tap and hold an empty space on the home screen. To go to the home screen from any screen, press the home button.

57

- Then you will see a screen that looks like the one below:

- You can perform any of the following actions:
    o **Add a screen**: To do this, swipe left until you see the plus/Add **(+)** icon.

After you add a screen, you can add app shortcuts to the newly added home screen. To do this, tap and hold the app icon on the applications screen and then select **Add shortcut to Home**.

o **Remove a screen**: To do this, swipe left until you see the home screen you want to remove. Then tap the **Delete** icon located on top of the screen you want to delete.

Delete icon

- **Change the order of the home screens:** To do this, tap and hold a screen and drag it to the edge of the screen until the page turns. When the home screen is in the right position, lift your finger.

Tap and hold the screen you want to move, then move it to the right edge or left edge of the screen until the page turns. When the screen is in right position lift your finger.

To easily access a home screen, you may consider setting it as your **main** home screen. Please see below to learn how.

o **Set a screen as a main home screen:** To do this, swipe left or right until the screen is visible and then tap the **Home button** located at the top of the screen. When a screen is your main home screen, the home screen button appears bold.

Tip: To access your main home screen at any point in time, press the dedicated home button .

- **Hello Bixby**: To access Bixby screen, swipe right. To enable or disable this feature, tap the status switch. To learn more about Bixby, please go to page 181.

Tip: To move out of a setting when you are done, tap the back button.

Hint: Do you want to increase the number of apps that appear in a row on the Home screen? If yes, then go to page 77 to learn more.

Add/Remove an app shortcut to the home screen
You can add apps/items to the home screen so that you can easily access them anytime.
To do this:
1. Access the app screen by swiping up the screen while on the home screen.
2. While in the app screen, tap and hold an app icon, and then select **Add shortcut to Home**.

66

3. To remove an app shortcut from the home screen, tap and hold the app icon you want to remove and then select **Remove shortcut**. Please note that removing an app icon from the home screen does not uninstall the app, it merely removes it from the home screen.

Managing the home screen widget

Widget is a small item that allows you to control an app in a special way. Widgets display information and invite the user to act in special ways.

To add a widget to a home screen:
1. While on the home screen, place your two fingers on the screen and then move them closer, or tap and hold an empty

space on the home screen. To go to the home screen from any screen, press the home button .

2. Tap on **Widgets** located at the bottom of the screen.

3. Swipe left or right to see the available widgets. Tap and hold a widget from the list of the widgets that appear, drag it to a home screen and release it.

4. To move a widget to a new location, tap, hold and drag the widget to the desired location. Tap outside the widget to save the changes.
5. To remove a widget from the home screen, tap and hold the widget and then select **Remove**.

6. To resize a resizable widget, touch and hold, then release the widget. Then drag the rectangular blue outline to the desired

size. Tap outside the widget to save the changes. *Please note that not all widgets can be resized.*

Managing the home screen theme

1. While on the home screen, place your two fingers on the screen and then move them closer, or tap and hold an empty space on the home screen. To go to the home screen from any screen, press the home button.
2. Tap on **Wallpapers and themes** located at the bottom of the screen.

3. Tap **Theme** located at the lower side of the screen, and then choose a theme. *Please note that you may need to agree to Terms and Conditions before you can access themes.*

Step 2   **Step 3**

4. To see all your themes, tap **VIEW ALL**.

5. To see more wallpapers, tap the back icon and browse the available themes.
6. When you have seen the theme you like, tap **Download** and then tap **Apply**.

Step A

Step B

Please note that visual elements such as colors, icons, and wallpapers, may change depending on the selected theme.

Managing the home screen wallpaper

This option allows you to change the wallpaper settings for the Home screen and the locked screen.

1. While on the home screen, place your two fingers on the screen and then move them closer, or tap and hold an empty space on the home screen. To go to the home screen from any screen, press the home button.
2. Tap on **Wallpapers and themes** located at the bottom of the screen.

3. Tap **Wallpapers.**
4. To see all your wallpapers, tap **VIEW ALL.**

5. Choose a wallpaper from the list of wallpapers that appear. Under **Set as Wallpaper**, choose an option. Then tap **Set as Wallpaper.**
6. To see more wallpapers, tap the back icon and browse the available wallpapers.
7. When you have seen the wallpaper you like, tap **Download** and then tap **Apply.**

8. Under **Set as Wallpaper**, choose an option. Then tap **Set as Wallpaper**.

Please note that you may be prompted while trying to apply a wallpaper, just read the information shown to you and agree if you like.

What about the screen grid?
The screen grid option allows you to choose the number of app icons that is displayed in a row on your home screen.
1. While on the home screen, place your two fingers on the screen and then move them closer, or tap and hold an empty

space on the home screen. To go to the home screen from any screen, press the home button 🏠.

2. Tap **Home screen settings**.
3. Tap **Home screen grid**.

4. Choose a dimension. 4x5 means there are four apps in a row and five apps in a column; 4x6 means there are four apps in a row and six apps in a column; and 5x5 means there are five apps in a row and five apps in a column.

5. When you are done picking a dimension, tap **Apply** (located at the top of the screen).

Tip: Alternatively, you can access the **home screen settings** by performing the following actions:

- While on the home screen, swipe up the screen to access the applications screen.

- Tap the menu icon and select **Settings**.

To create a folder of items/apps on the Home Screen:
1. From the home screen or applications screen, tap and hold an app, then drag and drop it onto another item/app's icon to create a folder.
2. Tap **Enter folder name** and enter a folder name.
3. To change the color of the folder, tap the color button
 and select a color.
4. To add another app, tap **ADD APPS** located at the bottom of the screen.

80

5. When you are done customizing a folder, tap anywhere outside of the folder or tap the **Done** button on the virtual keyboard.
6. To remove an app from a folder, tap the folder, and then long-tap the app you want to remove and drag it out of the folder.

Accessing and Managing Applications

To open an app:

1. From the home screen; swipe up from the bottom of the screen to access applications screen.
2. Tap on the app of your choice
3. To go back to the app grid screen, press the back button

Accessing Recently Opened or Running Applications

1. Tap on the recent button to show the recent apps window. This contains the list of all opened/running apps.

2. Tap on an app to launch it, or tap the **X** icon to close it. To close all opened apps, tap **CLOSE ALL** located at the bottom of the screen.

Tip: You can lock an app so that it does not get closed when you tap **CLOSE ALL.** To do this, tap the recent button and select the menu icon located at the top of the screen. Then select **Lock apps.**

Select the padlock icon next to the app window you want to lock and tap **DONE**. When the padlock icon is closed then the app window is locked.

*Please note that although a locked app window is not closed when you tap **CLOSE ALL**, you can still close it by swiping it to the right or left.*

Advice: Although your phone can run more than one app at a time, multitasking may cause hang-ups, freezing, memory problems, or additional power consumption. To avoid these, end all unused programs by closing the app.

Managing the applications screen

Selecting apps

You can select many apps to perform an action on all of them at the same time. To do this:
1. Tap and hold an app, and then tap **Select multiple items**.

2. Then select all apps you want, and choose an option at the top of the screen. If an option appears grey that means you can't use the option. For example, if your selection contains a folder, then the **Create folder** icon will appear grey because you can't put a folder inside another folder. Also, you can tap and hold an app in your selection to move them to another part of the screen. Or you can drag the selected apps up the screen to move them to the home screen and make them shortcuts.

Choose an option

Tip: If an app has a badge, you can clear this badge by following the method below.

Tap and hold the app with the badge and select **Clear badge.**

Please note that a badge is a notification number displayed on an app icon, e.g.

Showing the apps button

You can choose to show the apps button on the home screen. To do this:

1. While on the home screen, swipe up the screen to access the applications screen.

2. Tap the menu icon and select **Settings**.

3. Tap **Apps button** and then choose **Show Apps button.** Then tap **APPLY** located at the top of the screen.

89

Arranging Application Alphabetically

1. While on the home screen, swipe up the screen to access the application screen.

2. Tap the menu icon ⋮ next to the search bar.

3. Tap **Sort** and choose an option.

Note: If you choose to arrange your apps/folders alphabetically, the folders will appear first.

Hiding applications

If you don't want your kid to access sensitive apps on your phone, you can hide them. For example, if you don't want your children to access your shopping app, you can hide them. However, please note that people may still be able to see your hidden apps, if they are tech savvy and they know the way.

To hide apps:

1. While on home screen, swipe up the screen to access the applications screen.

2. Tap the menu icon ⋮ and select **Settings**.

3. Tap **Hide apps.** Then select the apps you want to hide and tap **APPLY** located at the top of the screen.

4. To unhide the apps, just repeat the steps 1 to 3 above and unselect the apps you have selected before. Then tap **APPLY** located at the top of the screen.

Managing Applications

You can force-stop a misbehaving app. In addition, you can clear cache/data to clear errors in an app or to save phone memory.

To force-stop an app:
1. Swipe down from the top of the screen and tap settings icon

2. Swipe up and tap **Apps**.
3. Tap the app to manage
4. To disable an app, tap the **DISABLE.** Disabling an app may make such an app unavailable. To enable an app, repeat steps

92

1 to 3 above and tap **ENABLE**. *Please note that you may not be able to disable some apps on your phone. For example, you may not be able to disable some apps that came with your phone.*

5. To force-stop an app, tap **FORCE STOP.** Force-stopping an app is useful when an app is misbehaving or when it refuses to close. To access a force-stopped app again, just relaunch the app from the application screen.

6. To clear the cache or data of an app, tap **Storage** and then tap **CLEAR DATA** or **CLEAR CACHE.** *Please note that clearing data may cause you to lose settings, files and all other stored information on the app. Only clear the data of an app if you want to start using it as a new app.*

Tip: If you don't see **Clear Data** in the step 6 above, then choose **Manage Storage.** When you choose **Manage Storage** option, you should be able to access Clear Data tab.

7. To manage the notification of an app, tap **Notifications** and choose an option.
8. To manage the permissions you have given to an app, scroll down and tap **Permissions** and choose an option.

Hint: If you see that an app is disturbing you with notifications and you want to quickly manage notification settings, just swipe down from the top of the screen and tap **NOTIFICATION SETTINGS.** Then use the status switch or setting icon next to each app to manage their notifications. To learn more about phone notifications, see page 97.

Managing the Navigation Bar

The navigation bar is the bar at the bottom of your device screen. This bar comprises of back icon, home icon and recent apps icon. Interestingly, you can hide or unhide this bar. To do this:

1. Swipe down from the top of the screen and tap settings icon ⚙.

2. Then tap on the search icon.

3. Type in **Navigation bar** into the search bar. The result filters as you type. Tap **Navigation bar** from the results that appear.
4. Choose an option from the Navigation bar settings screen.
5. To enable the **Show and hide button**, tap the status switch next to **Show and hide button.** When this is enabled you should be able to quickly hide the navigation bar by tapping the small dot icon.

To show the navigation bar after hiding it, swipe in from the bottom of the screen.

Managing Phone Notifications

Notifications consume battery and may be a source of disturbance occasionally. To manage notifications:

1. Swipe down from the top of the screen and tap settings icon

   ⚙

2. Then tap **Notifications**.

3. Use the status switch to manage notification for individual apps. To disable all notifications, tap the status switch next to **All apps** (located at the top of the screen.) To have an advanced management of notifications, tap **ADVANCED** and choose an app. You can use the advanced settings to manage apps that can give you notifications while **Do Not Disturb** (see page 281) is active.

Tips: To manage notification sound on your phone, swipe down from the top of the screen, and tap **Settings** ⚙ > **Sounds and vibration** > **Notification sounds** > **Messages notifications/Calendar notifications.** Then tap the status switch next to **ON** to disable notification sound. To change the notification sound, tap **Notification sound** and choose an option.

In addition, you can select whether you see notification details or notification icon only on lock screen. To do this, swipe down from the top of the screen, and tap **Settings** ⚙ > **Lock screen and security** > **Notifications.** Then tap the status switch next to **Notification icons only** to hide notifications details and show only the icon.

Furthermore, you can quickly manage a notification from the quick action menu. To do this, simply swipe down from the top of the screen and tap and hold a notification. Then choose an option and tap **DONE** to effect the changes. To view the detailed settings of a notification, select **DETAILS**.

Using the Multi Window/Split-Screen Function

Multi window is one of the coolest features of Samsung Galaxy Note 8. Multi window allows you to put two apps side by side. *However, it is important to note that not all apps support multi window feature.*

Using Multi Window feature:

Before you start using multi-window/split-screen, I will advise that you enable Recent button multi window feature. To do this:

1. Swipe down from the top of the screen and tap settings icon

    ⚙️

2. Tap **Advanced features.**
3. Scroll down and tap **Multi window**

4. Tap the status switch next to **Use Recents button.**

Note that when this option is enabled, you will be able to change the current app from full screen view to split-screen view by pressing and holding Recent button ⌐.

To use multi window feature:
1. Open an app that supports multi-screen (e.g. phone app).

2. Touch and hold the recent button ⌐ and then tap **APPS LIST.**

3. Choose an app from the list that appears.

4. Alternatively, tap the recent button ![] to open the list of recently used apps. Then tap the split-screen icon ![] on the app you want to split. The app will launch in the upper window and the other recently used apps that support multi window will display below the launched app. Swipe up or down (if necessary) and select the second app.

5. To adjust the size of an app window, tap the middle of the dividing line between the app windows (i.e. the straight line that appears between the two app windows) and drag it up or down. See the picture below.

6. To close an app opened in split-screen, tap the split-screen icon ▤ and then tap the **X** icon next to the app you want to close. See below.

If you can't see the **X** icon, then the app is locked. To unlock the app, tap the padlock icon.

7. To open another app in split-screen, tap the split-screen icon , tap **APP LIST** and then select an app.

8. To exit multi window view, tap and hold the split-screen icon .

Using the Multi Window Controls

When using apps in the split screen view, tap the middle of the dividing line between the app windows to access multi window options.

SETTINGS	🔍
SOFTWARE UPDATE	×
Tap here to update the firmware to the latest version and use the latest features.	

📶 **Connections**
Wi-Fi, Bluetooth, Data usage, Airplane mode

🔊 **Sounds and vibration**
Sounds, Vibration, Do not disturb

📋 **Notifications**
Block, allow, prioritize

< 🔍 Search   🎤

Tap this

No recent searches

109

The Multi Window Options

Icon	Function
1.	Tap this icon to move an app window to another part (usually the top part of the screen). When you tap this icon, a blue outline will appear. Adjust this blue outline as you like to resize the window. When you are done resizing, tap **DONE** to effect the changes. To disable this function, tap the middle of the dividing line between the app windows (see the picture on page 109) and select .
2.	Tap this icon to switch window positions i.e. move a lower app window to upper part of the screen and vice versa.
3.	Tap this to open an app in a pop-up windows or minimize an app.
4.	Tap this icon to close the currently active app.

Using the Minimize icon:

1. When using apps in the split-screen view, tap the middle of the dividing line between the app windows to access multi-window options.

	SETTINGS	Q
	SOFTWARE UPDATE	✕
	Tap here to update the firmware to the latest version and use the latest features.	
📄	**Connections** Wi-Fi, Bluetooth, Data usage, Airplane mode	
🔊	**Sounds and vibration** Sounds, Vibration, Do not disturb	
📋	**Notifications** Block, allow, prioritize	

⬆
Tap this

No recent searches

2. Tap the minimize icon ☐ to open the currently active app in a pop-up window; then tap and hold the upper part of the window next to the outline to drag the window from one part

of the screen to another. To resize it however, tap, hold and move the outline as you wish.

Tap and hold the upper part of the window (next to the outline) to move it to another part of the screen

Drag this outline to resize the window

Drag this outline to resize the window

3. Tap to minimize the app window to a small icon. This small icon can be dragged from one part of the screen to another when you tap, hold and move it.

4. To maximize the window to a full screen, tap

Understanding the Quick Settings menu

The Quick settings panel present on notification panel provides a quick access to your device functions such as Wi-Fi, allowing you to quickly turn them on or off.

Tip: The app icon that is currently active in Quick settings menu will appear bold, so if you want to know whether you have enabled a feature or not, just check it boldness. For example, if you want to know if Bluetooth is on, swipe down from the top of the screen and see if the Bluetooth icon appears bold.

To view additional Quick settings:

1. Swipe down from the top of the screen to display the Notification panel.

2. Drag down the double dash == icon to see more icons. This icon is located just below the Quick settings icons.

Tip: To have a robust view of the Quick settings icon, swipe down from the top of the screen using two fingers.

To customize the Quick settings that display:

1. Swipe down from the top of the screen using two fingers.

2. Tap the menu icon ⋮ located at the top of the screen.

3. Tap **Button order.**

4. Drag any of the icons to change their positions.

5. To add an app to the Quick settings panel, drag the app from lower section of the screen (the gray area) to the top section of the screen.

6. To remove an icon from the Quick settings panel, drag the app icon to the lower section of the screen (the gray area).

6. Tap **DONE** located at the top of the screen to save the changes.

7. To restore the icons' arrangement to the default arrangement, tap **RESET** and then tap **DONE.**

115

Tip: To change the number of app icons that appear in a row/column in Quick settings menu, repeat steps 1 and 2 above and then select **Button grid** and choose an option.

Customizing Your Phone

You can get more done with your phone by customizing it to match your preference.

To change your language
1. Swipe down from the top of the screen and select settings icon ⚙. Then scroll down and tap **General management.**
2. Tap **Language and input.**
3. Tap **Language**.
4. Tap **Add language**.
5. If you want to access a more robust list of languages, tap the menu icon ⋮ and then tap **All languages.**

6. Select a language from the list. If your chosen language is spoken in more than one country/region, select a country/region for your chosen language.

7. Using the v-like icon next to a language, tap and drag your preferred language to the number one position in the

language list. Then tap **Apply** to set the language as the default language.

> Tap APPLY to save changes
>
> Tap and drag this icon to rearrange the languages

8. To delete a language, tap **DELETE** located at the top of the screen and tap the language you want to delete. Then select **DELETE** and tap **OK**. Please see below for details.

Selecting the Default Keyboard

1. Swipe down from the top of the screen and select settings icon . Then scroll down and tap **General management**.
2. Tap **Language and input.**
3. Tap **Default Keyboard** and then choose a keyboard. Please note that if you have not downloaded extra keyboards from Google Play Store, you may just see only two options.

I will advise that you go to Google Play Store to download more keyboard(s). Just open Google Play Store app and search for **Keyboard.** Then choose a beneficial keyboard from the options that appear. After you have downloaded and installed a keyboard, then perform the following actions:

1. Swipe down from the top of the screen and select settings icon ⚙. Then scroll down and tap **General management.**
2. Tap **Language and input.**
3. Tap **On-screen keyboard**

4. Tap **Manage keyboards**.
5. Tap the status switch next to the keyboard you just installed. In this case, I have just downloaded and installed **SwiftKey Keyboard** from Google Play store. Please note that you can't disable Samsung Keyboard. It is enabled by default and it appears there is nothing you can do about this.

6. Then tap the back button until you see **Language and Input** screen. Then tap **Default keyboard**, and choose an option.

Hint: Your device comes preloaded with Samsung Keyboard, to customize this keyboard to your taste, swipe down from the top of the screen, and tap **Settings** ⚙ **> General management > Language and input > On-Screen Keyboard > Samsung keyboard.** Then tap any of the on-screen options. I will advise that you go through these options serially in order to have the best keyboard experience.

In addition, to change the language of your keyboard to the one you like, swipe down from the top of the screen, and tap **Settings** > **General management** > **Language and input** > **On-Screen Keyboard** > **Samsung keyboard** > **Languages and types** > **MANAGE INPUT LANGUAGES.** Then tap the status switch next to the language you want to activate.

123

Hint: While using the keyboard, you can quickly change from one language to another by swiping the space bar on the virtual keyboard to right or left.

Set the Current Time and Date

Your device is built to update its time automatically, but you may need to manually set your time for one reason or the other. To manually set the time and date:

1. Swipe down from the top of the screen and select settings icon . Then scroll down and tap **General management.**
2. Tap **Date and time.**

3. To ensure that the time on your device is updated automatically, move the switch next to **Automatic date and time** to On.
4. To set the time on your device manually or prevent your device from updating the time automatically, move the switch next to **Automatic date and time** to Off, and then edit the time and date as you desire.
5. To manage the time zone settings, move the switch next to **Automatic date and time** to Off and then tap **Select time zone.**
6. To use a 24 hours' time setting for your device, move the switch next to **Use 24-hour format** to On.

Note: When the status switch is on, it will appear bold.

```
< CALENDAR SETTINGS
First day of week
Local default
Show week numbers          ← The status switch is off
Hide declined events       ← The status switch is on
```

To Control Sounds and Vibrations

1. Swipe down from the top of the screen and select settings icon ⚙.
2. Tap **Sounds and vibration** and tap an option. For example, to mute the sound on your phone, tap **Sound mode** and then tap **Mute.**

Adjusting the Volume of Your Phone

To adjust the volume of your phone, press the **Volume key**. The volume key is the long key located at the left side of your phone (when the phone is facing you).

Adjusting the Brightness of the Display
1. Swipe down from the top of the screen using your two fingers. Then drag the slider under the Quick action icons to adjust the brightness.

Hint: The brightness level of the display will affect how quickly the device consumes battery power. I will advise that you turn it reasonably low if you are very serious about saving your battery.

To Set a Screen Lock Password or PIN

You can lock your phone by activating the screen lock feature.

Note: Once you set a screen lock, your phone will require an unlock code each time you turn it on or unlock the touch screen.

1. Swipe down from the top of the screen and tap settings icon .
2. Tap **Lock screen and security** and then **Screen lock type**.
3. Tap a screen lock type you like.
4. If you choose **Password or PIN**, then enter the password/PIN you like and follow the onscreen instructions

to complete the setup. In addition, you may choose **Pattern** or **Swipe**. If you don't want a lock screen, tap **None**.

Tip: You may also use your face, fingerprint or iris to lock your phone. More on this in the next section (see page 134).

Entering a text

You can enter a text by selecting characters on the virtual keypad or by speaking words into the microphone using a voice command app.

To enter a text:
1. Enter a text by selecting the corresponding alphabets, symbols or numbers.
2. You can use any of the following keys:

Please note that the on-screen keyboard on your phone may be different from the one shown below. This is because the on-screen keyboard you see depends on the text input field you selected. The one shown below is the one you should see when you want to compose a text message.

Number	Function
1.	**Predictive text bar** **Tip**: As you type, your phone will give you text suggestions, the most likely suggestions will appear in blue in the predictive text bar. To use the suggestion that appears in blue, (the suggestion that appears at the center), tap the space bar. To use a different suggestion, tap on it.
2.	Tap on this to see more predictive texts.
3.	Clear your input/backspace
4.	Start a new line.
5.	Tap this icon to select a new keyboard type
6.	**Space bar**: you can swipe right, or swipe left to switch between input languages. To add input

		language, please go to page 123.
7.		**Option tab**: when you press and hold this button, you will gain an access to a list of icons.
8.		Switch between Number/Symbol mode and ABC mode
9.		Change case

Hint: When you press and hold the option tab, you will gain an access to the following:

```
 7   6   5   4   3   2   1
```

1. **Keyboard settings:** Tap this to access the keyboard settings.
2. **One-handed keyboard**: Tap this to be able to control the virtual keyboard using one hand. When you tap the **One-handed keyboard** button, you will see a keyboard that looks like the one below.

Tap this to exit One-handed keyboard

Tap this to move keyboard to the left

3. **Emoticon**: Tap this to add emoticons to your texts.
4. **Clipboard:** Tap this to add an item from the clipboard. After using an item on the clipboard, tap the arrow icon (located at the bottom of the screen) to exit.
5. **Live Message:** Tap this to compose live message.
6. **Pen Input:** Tap this icon to write using S Pen instead of typing. When you are done writing and you want to exit, tap keyboard icon.
7. **Voice input**: Enter text by voice.

Tip: To learn how to manage the on-screen keyboard, please see page 122. When you select two or more languages, you can switch between the input languages by swiping to the left or right on the space key.

To Copy and Paste a Text

While you are entering a text, you can use the copy and paste feature to use the copied text in another application.

1. Tap and hold a word to display copy options. The icons below will show up after selecting a text or texts.

   Select all Cut Copy Paste More ⬅ **Tap this icon to see more options**

2. Drag ◐ or ◑ to select more texts.
3. Select **Copy** icon to copy, or select **Cut** icon to cut the text onto the clipboard.
4. In another application or where you want to paste the text, tap and hold the text input field.
5. Select **Paste** icon to insert the text from the clipboard into the text input field. You can also tap and hold the option tab (see page 130) and then select the clipboard icon 📋 to access the clipboard for more paste options.

Using the Voice Typing

1. Tap and hold the option tab (see page 130), and then select 🎤.
2. Speak your text. Your device types as you speak.
3. To pause the voice typing, tap the screen.
4. To manage the voice typing option, swipe down from the top of the screen, and tap **Settings** ⚙ > **General management** and tap **Language and input**. Tap **On-Screen keyboard** and tap **Samsung voice input**.

5. To exit the voice typing, tap the arrow icon ↓ (located at the bottom of the screen). Alternatively, you can also tap **X** icon to exit the voice typing.

Using The Special Features

Samsung Galaxy Note 8 came with special features that differentiate it from other smartphones. I will now explain how to use these features.

Using the Fingerprint Feature

One of the cool features on Samsung Galaxy Note 8 is Fingerprint. It allows you to unlock applications without entering boring passwords.

Registering your Fingerprint

Before you can start using your fingerprint on your device, you will need to first register your fingerprint. You have the chance of registering up to three fingerprints. In addition, you also have the option of registering a password as a backup. To do this:

1. Swipe down from the top of the screen and select settings icon ⚙.
2. Tap **Lock screen and security**.
3. Tap **Fingerprint scanner**.
4. Read the on-screen tips and tap **Continue**.
5. Tap an alternative lock method and follow the prompts. You will need this alternative lock method in some instances. If

you have set a lock screen before, then you just need to enter the lock PIN/Password/Pattern.

6. Place one of your fingers on the fingerprint reader located beside the phone camera at the back of the phone, then lift it when the fingerprint is detected and read. You may need to repeat this several times.

Fingerprint scanner

7. To add another fingerprint, tap **Add** and follow the prompts.
8. When you are done adding your fingerprints, tap **Done.**
9. Then select the display option for notifications on the lock screen. You can use this option to customize how notifications appear on your phone while the phone is locked. Tap **Done** after selecting your desired option.

Renaming Fingerprints

1. Swipe down from the top of the screen and select settings icon .
2. Tap **Lock screen and security**.
3. Tap **Fingerprint scanner**.
4. Unlock the screen using the preset screen lock method and tap **NEXT**.
5. Tap the fingerprint you want to rename. For example, tap **Fingerprint 1.**

6. Enter a new name, and then tap **Rename**.

Tip: When renaming your fingerprint, make sure you use the name of the finger you registered. For example, you can use the name **Index finger** or **Forefinger**. This prevents unnecessary confusions.

Deleting Fingerprints

1. Swipe down from the top of the screen and select settings icon .
2. Tap **Lock screen and security**.
3. Tap **Fingerprint scanner**.

137

4. Unlock the screen using the preset screen lock method and tap **NEXT**.
5. Touch and hold the fingerprint you want to delete, and then tap **Remove**.

Setting a Screen Lock with Fingerprint

You can lock the screen with your fingerprint instead of using a pattern, PIN, or password.

1. Swipe down from the top of the screen and select settings icon .
2. Tap **Lock screen and security**.
3. Tap **Screen lock type**.
4. Unlock the screen using the preset screen lock method and tap **NEXT**.
5. Tap the status switch next to **Fingerprint.**

138

Using Fingerprints to Sign In to Accounts

Apart from using your fingerprint to unlock your device, you can also use it to access online features.

1. Swipe down from the top of the screen and select settings icon ⚙.
2. Tap **Lock screen and security**.
3. Tap **Fingerprint scanner**. Then do any of the following:
   a. Tap **Samsung Pass** to access your online accounts/apps using your fingerprint. To get started with this feature, just tap Samsung Pass and follow the prompts.
   b. Tap **Samsung Pay** to use your fingerprint for secured and fast payments with the Samsung Pay app.

139

Samsung Pay is not available in some locations in the world.

c. Tap the switch next to **Fingerprint unlock** to enable or disable fingerprint security.

Troubleshooting the Fingerprint Scanner

If the fingerprint scanner is not responding, try any of the following:

1. Remove any phone case that may be covering the fingerprint reader located at the back of the phone.
2. Ensure that you are not using the tip of your fingerprint. Make sure to cover the entire Fingerprint reader with your finger.
3. If your finger has scars, try using another finger, this is because your device may not recognize fingerprints that are affected by wrinkles or scars.
4. Make sure you use the particular finger you use to register your fingerprint.
5. Make sure that your finger and the surface of the fingerprint scanner are clean and dry.

Iris Scanner

You can lock and unlock your phone using your iris.

1. Swipe down from the top of the screen and select settings icon ⚙.
2. Tap **Lock screen and security**.
3. Tap **Iris scanner**. You may need to setup an alternative lock screen method or enter your lock screen information if you have already setup a lock screen.
4. Read the on-screen tips and tap **OK/Continue**.
5. Hold the phone 10 inches to 14 inches from your face. Make sure you are not wearing glasses. Follow the prompts to complete the registration.
6. After the registration, you will see some information telling you more about the Iris scanner. Read this information and tap next icon > located at the bottom of the screen. Finally tap **OK** to go to Iris setting page.

> **SELECT A MASK**
>
> Add your own style to iris scanning. Go to Settings > Lock screen and security > Iris Scanner > Preview screen mask.

7. On the Iris setting page, tap an option to enable/disable it. To know what each option stands for, read the information under the option.

8. To remove Iris data, tap **Remove iris data** and tap **Remove**.

Troubleshooting the Iris Scanner

If the Iris scanner is not responding, try any of the following:

1. Remove any screen protector that may be covering the iris camera, LED sensor, or proximity sensor located above your screen. See page 7-8 for the picture of these sensors/camera.
2. Ensure that you are not wearing glasses.
3. Ensure that you are not trying to use the Iris scanner under the direct sunlight.

Water Resistance

Another feature that makes Samsung Galaxy Note 8 unique is the water resistivity. You don't have to worry that your phone is going to get wet when you are inside the rain or a bathroom. To know more about water resistivity, please go to page 44.

The S Pen

One of the features that make using Galaxy Note 8 very interesting is the stylus pen. You can use S pen as you use a normal writing pen. In this section of the guide, I will be telling you how to use your S pen like a pro.

Removing the S Pen

To remove the S Pen:
1. Push the S Pen inward until it pops out of the device.

S Pen

2. Then gently slide the S Pen out using the notch on the end of the S Pen.

S Pen Layout

Number	Function
1.	**S Pen Head:** Push this head inward to remove the S Pen from Note 8.

2.		S Pen Body
3.		**S Pen Button**: You can press this button to launch the Air Command (see page 149). In addition, you can use this button to erase what you have written. Just press the S Pen button and move the tip of the S pen over whatever you want to erase.
4.		**S Pen Tip**: This tip allows you to write on the surface of your device. This tip is removable.

Tip: You may customize the S Pen features as you like. To do this, swipe down from the top of the screen and tap **Settings** > **Advanced Features > S Pen.**

Use these options to customize S Pen as you like

147

S Pen and Air View

One of the cool features with the S pen is the Air View. Air View allows you to view more information about an item just by hovering your S Pen over it.

For example, you can hover the S Pen over a date in your calendar app to preview the events for that day. In addition, you can hover over an icon to view the icon's name or description. The trick is to hover your S Pen tip over whatever you want to learn more about. Please note that the preview function may not be available in some cases.

In addition, please note that you may need to enable Air View. To do this, swipe down from the top of the screen and tap **Settings** > **Advanced Features** > **S Pen** >**Air view**

S Pen and Air Command

Air Commands are set of options that appear when you remove the S Pen from your device. These options give more usability to the S Pen.

To access the Air Command:

- Remove the S Pen from its holder by pushing it inwards and letting it pop out. The Air Command menu will open automatically. If you already have taken the S Pen out, tap the S Pen icon ![icon] (located at the middle edge of the screen) to access the Air Command. Another way to open the Air Command is to hold the S Pen near the screen so that the pointer appears, then press the S Pen button (see page 146/147) once.

The screenshot below shows the Air Command options.

```
Create note ———— 1
View all notes ———— 2
Smart select ———— 3
                 ———— 4
Screen write
                 ———— 5
Live message
                 ———— 6
Translate        ———— 7
                 ———— 8
```

1. **Create Note**: Tap this using your S Pen to launch the Note app.
2. **View all notes**: Tap this to access all your notes.
3. **Smart Select**: Smart Select allows you to extract parts of an image. You can use this feature to extract out texts from an image. To use Smart select:
   a. Navigate to the page you want to capture, and then tap **Smart select** using the S Pen. Tap **Confirm** if you agree with the terms and conditions.
   b. Tap a shape at the top of the screen, and then drag a box with the S Pen to select content. In this example **Rectangle** is selected.

   c. Draw a rectangle around the area you wish to select.
   d. Tap **Auto select** or **Extract text**
   e. Tap **Save.** The saved image should be in your gallery.
4. **Screen Write:** This allows you to capture screenshots and write or draw on them.
5. **Live message:** Tap this to write and share live messages.

6. **Translate:** When this is selected, hover the S Pen over a word to see it translated into another language and listen to its pronunciation. To use the translation feature:
    a. While on the Air Command screen, tap **Translate**.
    b. Tap the Source and Target languages to change them to the desired language(s).

Target language

English ⇄ English ✕ ——— Tap this icon to close this feature

Source language

   c. Hover the S Pen over a word to see its translation.
   d. Tap the voice icon 🔊 to hear the word pronounced in the source language.
   e. Tap **X** to close this feature.

7. **Bixby Vision:** Tap this to access **Bixby Vision** (see page 202).
8. **Air Command Settings:** This allows you to customize S Pen settings.

Tip: You may be wondering how do you access **Add shortcuts** tab if it is not showing. To access **Add shortcuts** tab; while on the Air Command page, swipe up using the S Pen.

If "Add schortcuts" option is not showing, swipe up using your S Pen (see the arrow) to bring it into view.

Add shortcuts allows you to add or remove items from the Air Command menu. To add a shortcut:

    a. While on the Air Command screen tap **Add shortcuts**.

b. Tap the apps you would like to add.

c. To delete an app shortcut, tap the minus icon next to the app you want to delete.

d. Tap the back button to save the changes.

Hint: You can quickly remove an icon from the Air Command screen. To do this, using the S pen, tap and hold an icon and drag it to **Remove** located at the top of the screen.

Using the S Pen, tap and drag the icon you want to remove to the top of the screen. In this case, I am trying to remove Bixby Vision icon.

Using the S Pen and the handwriting panel

You can write something on the writing field of supported apps, and your device will automatically convert your written words to text. To do this:

1. Open an app and hover the S Pen over the text field (where you want to type information) until the **Handwriting to text** icon appears.

2. Tap Handwriting to text icon and begin to write in the writing field that appears. Your entries will be converted to text.

3. To delete a text, strikethrough the handwritten text. In addition, you can edit the converted text using your keyboard.

S Pen and Screen Off Memo

Quick memos allow you to write without turning your device on. To create a screen off memo:

1. Detach the S Pen while the screen is off to access screen off memo. If you have detached the S Pen already, then tap the screen while pressing the S Pen button (see page 146/147) to access the screen off memo.

2. Write on the screen.

3. To go to another page or open a new page, tap the new page icon .

4. Tap **SAVE IN NOTES** located at the top of the screen to save your memo to the Samsung Notes app. Alternatively, to save the memo, just replace the S Pen into its slot.

5. To pin a note to **Always On Display**, tap the pin icon and then tap **Pin To Always On Display**.

6. To erase a word, select the eraser icon , and move the tip of your S pen over what you want to erase. Alternatively, to erase a word, press the S Pen button (see page 146/147) and move the tip of the S pen over whatever you want to erase.

7. To delete the note, tap the back button ⬅ and then select **Discard**.

If not enabled, please note that you may need to enable screen off memo to use it. To do this, swipe down from the top of the screen and tap **Settings** ⚙ > **Advanced Features > S Pen > Screen off memo**.

Changing the tip of your S Pen

You can replace the tip of the S Pen with the included pen tip removal tool.

To change the pen tip:
1. Grasp the pen tip with the included tweezers (the metal-like object included with your phone) and pull it straight out.
2. Insert the base of the new tip into the pen opening and push it in until it locks into place.

Tweezers and pen tips

Using the Always on Feature

The Always On feature allows you to display information, such as a clock, calendar, or image, on the screen when it is turned off. I personally love the fact that you can check the time with this feature even if the screen is off.

1. Swipe down from the top of the screen and select settings icon ✱.
2. Tap **Lock screen and security**.
3. Scroll down and tap **Always on display**.

4. Tap On/Off switch to enable or disable Always on Display.

159

When you enable **Always on Display**, you can access the following:

a. **Content to show**: This feature allows you to choose the content to show when the screen is off. See the screenshot below.

b. **Clock style/Calendar style/Image**: This option allows you to choose the clock style, calendar style, image, or Edge clock. When you select an option, please note that you will need to tap **Apply** located at the top of the screen to effect changes. Note that you may not be able to choose a clock, image or calendar to display if you choose **Home button** only in section **a.** above.

Tip: To change the color of the clock or the calendar, tap the color icon ▣ and choose a color.

    c. **Show Always**: When this is enabled, the Always on Display is active every time. To customize when Always On will be active, tap the status switch next to **Show Always** and set a schedule.

d. **About Always on Display**: Tap this to view the current software version and license information.

Good news: One interesting thing about Always On option is that it consumes a very low amount of energy.

Live Message

This option allows you to record an animated message. It gives an interesting look to your written messages.
To use live message:
1. Remove the S Pen from its holder by pushing it inwards and letting it pop out. The Air Command menu will open automatically. If you already have taken the S Pen out, tap the S Pen icon (located at the middle edge of the

screen) to access the Air Command. Another way to open the Air Command is to hold the S Pen near the screen so that the pointer appears, then press the S Pen button (see page 146/147) once.

2. Tap **Live message** icon.

3. Then begin to write.

Fast Battery Charging

One of the cool features on Samsung Galaxy Note 8 is Fast Battery Charging. With this feature, your device can get 50% of battery power in about 45 minutes. You can learn how to use this feature by going to page 21.

Using the Edge Screen on Samsung Galaxy Note 8

The Edge screen transforms the way you handle Samsung Galaxy Note 8. Edge panels can be used to access apps, tasks, contacts and more. To access the Edge panel, drag the Edge panel handle located at the Edge of the screen. To access more Edge items, swipe again from the Edge of the screen.

Swipe this handle

To access Edge panel settings, tap the settings ⚙ icon located at the bottom of the screen (this setting icon appears while viewing the Edge options).

Using the Edge Panel

The Edge Panel allows you to use the Edge screen in a special way. To manage the Edge panel:
1. Swipe down from the top of the screen and select settings icon   . Then tap **Display** tab.
2. Scroll down and tap **Edge Screen**.
3. Tap **Edge Panels**.
4. To download exciting panels, tap **Download** located at the top of the screen and tap the Edge panel you want to download. Then tap **Install** to install your downloaded panel.

To go back to the Edge panel screen, tap the back button ←.

To see your newly installed panel, navigate to the **Edge Panels** screen and swipe left.

Swipe left to see the newly installed panel. In this case, calendar panel is the newly installed panel.

5. To uninstall an Edge panel that you don't like, tap the menu icon located at the top of the Edge panel's screen and select **Uninstall**. Then select the minus icon (--) located at the top of the panel you want to uninstall. When prompted, tap **OK**. Please note that the uninstall button may not be available if you have not installed any Edge panel from the Edge panel store.

6. There are some Edge panels that allow you to edit them. To edit an editable panel, just tap **EDIT** next to the panel you want to edit. Please note that you may need to enable a panel before you can edit it. To learn how to enable a panel, please go to step 7.

Editable panel

Then tap and hold an item and move it to the Edge screen. To remove an item, tap the minus icon. To rearrange the icons, tap and drag the icon(s) to a new location. See the picture below.

[Figure: Screenshot of APPS EDGE screen with annotations:
- "Tap and drag any of these icons to move it to another location"
- "Tap this minus icon to remove an app from the edge screen"
- "Tap and hold an icon and drag it to the right side of the screen"]

Although, *Apps Edge* has been used in the example above, you can also manage People Edge in similar way. In addition, please note that there is a maximum number of items you can add to the Edge screen.

7. To enable an Edge panel or select the Edge panel that you want to see on the Edge screen, just tap the circle on top of the panel. To disable/remove a panel, simply unselect the circle.

170

8. To disable an Edge panel totally, tap the status switch next to **ON**. Please note that when you disable Edge Panel, the Edge handle will disappear.

Note: If you download many Edge panels, you may not be able to access all these panels at once on your Edge screen. You may not be able to use more than nine Edge panels at once. To select the Edge panels that you want to access, simply follow the step 7 above.

Using the Edge Lighting

This feature allows you to set the Edge screen to light up when you receive calls or notifications.

1. Swipe down from the top of the screen and select settings icon . Tap **Display** tab.
2. Scroll down and tap **Edge Screen**.

3. Tap **Edge Lighting**.
4. Move the switch to **on** position.

5. Select when to show the Edge lighting. If you want Edge Lighting to be active every time, then select **Always**.
6. Tap **Manage notifications** to select those apps that will work with Edge Lighting.

[Screenshot: Manage Notifications screen with app list]

Tap the status switch next to an app to enable the Edge lighting notification for that app

Note: It appears that not all notifications may be received as Edge lighting.

Tip: To customize the color, the size, or the transparency of the Edge lighting, tap the **Advanced Settings** and then choose an option.

[Screenshots: Edge Lighting settings and Advanced Settings screens]

Step a — Advanced settings

Step b — Choose an option

174

Reordering the Edge Screen Panel

1. Swipe down from the top of the screen and select settings icon . Tap **Display** tab.
2. Scroll down and tap **Edge Screen**.
3. Tap **Edge Panels**.
4. Tap the menu icon located at the top of the screen and tap **REORDER**.
5. Tap and hold the Re-order icon (<>) on an Edge screen panel and drag it to the desired position. Make sure that the panels you use most are in the first 3 or 4 panels so that you can access them faster.

6. Tap back icon to save the changes.

Managing the Edge Panel Handle Settings/Changing the Edge Panel Location

Edge panel handle settings allows you to change the position of Edge panel and more.

1. Swipe down from the top of the screen and select settings icon . Tap **Display** tab.

176

2. Scroll down and tap **Edge Screen**.
3. Tap **Edge Panels**.
4. Tap the menu icon ⋮ located at the top of the screen and select **Handle Settings.**
5. Under **Position** tab, tap the side you would like the panel to appear on.
6. To change the size of Edge panel, drag the slider next to **SIZE**.
7. To change the transparency of Edge panel, drag the slider next to **Transparency.**
8. To move the Edge panel handle to another part of the screen, just tap and drag the Edge handle anchor (the small V-shape icon).

Tip: To let your phone alert you when you access Edge panel, tap the switch next to **Vibration**.

Using People Edge

People Edge gives you the opportunity to quickly access your favorite contacts from Edge Panel.

To manage People Edge:

1. Swipe down from the top of the screen and select settings icon . Tap **Display** tab.
2. Scroll down and tap **Edge Screen**.
3. Tap **Edge Panels**.

4. Tap **EDIT** under **People Edge.** If you can't see the Edit button, then People Edge is disabled. To enable People Edge, simply tap the small circle ◯ located on top of this panel.
5. Tap **SELECT CONTACT** and select all the contacts you want by tapping them. Tap **DONE** to save the changes. You should now be able to access the selected contacts when you access the Edge panel.

6. To remove a contact from the People Edge, tap the minus icon next to the contact you want to remove.

The Bixby

Bixby is a trained virtual assistant that has been built to answer questions, and let you interact with your phone in a special way. Bixby is divided into three parts:

1. Bixby Home
2. Bixby Vision
3. Bixby Voice

This section of the guide will show you how to manage Bixby like a pro.

Getting started with Bixby

You will need to setup Bixby when you first start using your device and you will learn how to do that in this section of the guide. To setup this voice assistant:

1. Press the Bixby button (the button next to volume button at the side of the phone).

2. If you see a screen telling you to update Bixby, simply tap **UPDATE.**

3. Tap **Next.**

4. Choose a language for Bixby Voice and tap **Confirm**.

5. Read the terms and conditions. If you agree to all the terms and conditions, tap **I have read and agreed to all** and then tap **NEXT**.

6. Follow the onscreen instructions to setup and register your voice so that Bixby can recognize your voice.

7. To manage a card, tap the menu icon next to it. Then tap an option.

8. To adjust Bixby settings, tap the menu icon located at top of the screen and tap **Settings**. Then choose an option.

To choose which card is displayed to you on the home page, tap **Cards** and use the status switch to turn off/on a card.

185

Tip: To customize the type of briefing you receive on the Bixby home page, tap the menu icon next to the briefing card and select **Customize content.**

Then choose the categories you want to receive information about.

Tap the back icon to save the changes.

186

Bixby Home

After the initial setup discussed above, you can access the Bixby Home by pressing the Bixby button (the button next to the volume button at the side of the phone). Alternatively, swipe right while on Home screen to access Bixby Home.

Bixby Voice

Bixby voice allows you to interact with Bixby using your voice.

Speaking to Bixby

One of the ways you will interact with Bixby is by speaking to it. The other way will be to just type command into the search bar and hit **Go**.

To get Bixby into action, you will need to get its attention. To do that, perform any of the actions below:

1. Press the Bixby button located next to the volume button at the side of your phone and speak your command while still pressing it.

2. Alternatively, you can get Bixby's attention by saying **Hi Bixby!** However, you may need to enable this feature before you can put it to use. To enable **Hi Bixby** function:

- Swipe in from the left edge of the screen while on the Home screen.

- Tap the menu icon ⋮ located at top of the screen and tap **Settings**.

← **Menu icon**

- Scroll down and tap **Voice wake-up.** Then tap the status switch next to **ON**.

- If you want to increase the sensitivity of Bixby to the wake word, drag the slider under **Wake-up sensitivity** to medium or high position.

When Bixby is activated, it will respond by displaying a small action box on the screen. Bixby will then give you an answer.

In addition, occasionally, you may notice that the question you asked Bixby is different from what it types into the action box. What Bixby types into the action box is what it thinks you have said.

Tip: You can train Bixby to recognize your voice, to do this:

- Swipe in from the left edge of the screen while on the Home screen.

- Tap the menu icon located at top of the screen and tap **Settings**.

- Tap **Enhanced voice recognition** and follow the onscreen instructions.

What about Typing?

The interesting thing is that Bixby can also listen when you command it using your onscreen keyboard. You can type in command and get a similar result just as you will get by speaking to it. This is a great feature especially if you can't speak to Bixby for one reason or the other e.g. if you are in a noisy place or your microphone is not working properly.

To use the Bixby typing feature:

- Press the Bixby button (located next to the volume button) for two seconds or say "**Hi Bixby**".
- Tap **Full Screen.**

190

- Tap the search bar located at the top of the screen and type your command. Wait for a reply.

Tip: If you are stuck and you don't know what to ask Bixby, you can use the typing menu to get some ideas. To do this, simply type a keyword into the search menu and scroll through the suggestions. For example, if you are looking for ideas on how to use Bixby with the Email app, just tap the text menu and key in **email**. Then scroll through the search results to see example commands.

Type a keyword and scroll through suggested commands.

Using Bixby to Open Apps or Programs

One of those things you will want to use Bixby to do is accessing your apps. You can quickly open an app by saying **Open** and then mention the name of the app. For example, to open settings, say or type **Open settings.** To open calculator, say **Open calculator**.

You may also say **Launch settings** instead of **Open settings.**

In addition, you may give a more specific command like **Open notification settings** to go to notification settings. Say **Launch Wi-Fi Settings** to open the Wi-Fi settings. To turn off airplane mode, say **Turn off airplane mode** and so on.

192

Using Bixby with Calendar

One of the fantastic features that Bixby can do for you is making an appointment. This personal assistant is fully integrated with your device Calendar making it easy for it to make appointments.

With just few commands, you can get Bixby to put an event or appointment into your Calendar. **To do this:**

1. Press the Bixby button located next to the volume button at the side of your phone and speak your command while still pressing it. Alternatively, say **Hi Bixby!**

2. Say whatever you want to include in the Calendar. For example, you can say any of the following:

   - Appointment with Clinton for Monday at 1 p.m.

   - Be in a conference with John by 10 a.m. on Sunday.

   - Remind me to fix my car at 9 p.m. tonight. Please note that you can also say all the examples given above in other ways, the most important thing is to get Bixby to understand what you are saying.

   - When it has got the information, the Calendar app will appear. You can then say **Yes** if you are satisfied with the response. If not, say **No**.

In addition, you can check how your calendar looks like. To do this, click the microphone button and say, "**What is on my calendar today?**" Or say, "**any appointment today**?" Or just any variant. Note that you can also ask Bixby about your calendar for a day in the future. To do this, say "**Any appointment tomorrow**" or say, "**Any appointment on November 1st.**"

Note: In case, Bixby sets a wrong appointment, you can edit it using your on-screen keyboard instead of trying to speak another word to it. Editing any misinformation with keyboard appears smarter and faster.

In addition, instead of speaking, you may type any of the commands mentioned above into the search box to get a similar result.

Using Bixby to Set Reminders

There are probably many things going through your mind, and it will be quite interesting if you can get a personal assistant to assist in remembering some of your duties. Fortunately, Bixby can help you in this regard.

To set a reminder using Bixby:

1. Press the Bixby button located next to the volume button at the side of your phone and speak your command while still pressing it. Alternatively, say **Hi Bixby!**

2. Say whatever you want to set a reminder for. For example, you can say the following:

- Remind me to fix the car by 3 p.m.

- Remind me to drop the cake at the restaurant.

- Remind me to pick my daughter at 4 p.m.

- Remind me to call Clinton at 1 p.m., and so on.

Please note that it is probably not compulsory that you put **remind** in every statement as I did above. But I will advise that you to do so whenever you can. This is because it will help Bixby to easily get what you are saying and avoid any confusion.

Note: In case, Bixby sets a wrong reminder, you can edit it using your on-screen keyboard instead of trying to speak another word to it. Editing any misinformation with keyboard appears smarter and faster.

Using Bixby with Alarm

You can also set an alarm using this personal assistant. **To do this**:

1. Repeat the first step mentioned above.

2. Say the time for alarm. For example, you can say: "**set an alarm for 1 p.m. every Wednesday**" or "**alarm for 1 p.m. every Wednesday**" or "**set an everyday alarm for 2 p.m.**" or "**set an alarm for 1 p.m. on 24th of October**".

3. When it has grabbed the information, the alarm will appear, and it will tell you that it has set the alarm.

Using Bixby with Clock

You can ask Bixby what your local time is. In addition, it can also tell you the time in a specific place.

1. Press the Bixby button located next to the volume button at the side of your phone and speak your command while still pressing it. Alternatively, say **Hi Bixby!**

2. Then say, "**What is the time?**" or say, "**what is the time in New York?**"

Using Bixby to Get Flight Information

You can also use this virtual assistant to get information about a flight. This is a smarter way to know when an airplane will take off.

For example, you can say **Flight status of Delta 400** to get the flight information about this flight.

Using Bixby with Weather App

To know about the weather condition of a place, just say "**What's the weather going to be today?**". You may also know about the weather condition of a place by asking "**What is the weather of New York today?**"

Using Bixby with Mail App

You can instruct Bixby to compose an email for you. To do this:

1. Press the Bixby button located next to the volume button at the side of your phone and speak your command while still pressing it. Alternatively, say **Hi Bixby!**

2. Then give the command. For example, you can say:

    - Send an email to Clinton.

    - Send an email to Clinton and Steve.

    - Search for emails from Clinton.

    - Search for emails from Steve and mark them all as important.

Please note that you will usually have to include one or more information before you send the email. For example, you may need to type the body of the email yourself.

Tip: You can get example commands to help you use the email app like a pro. To do this, please refer to the **tip** on page 191.

Using Bixby with Map App

You can also use the Bixby to search the map. This virtual assistant is fully integrated with the Map app on your device. **To get how the map of a place looks like**:

1. Repeat the first step above.

2. Then say the map of an area you want to get. For example, you may say:

    - Map of Seattle.

    - Show me the map of Seattle.

What about Math?

Bixby can also help you with some mathematical calculations and conversions. For example, you can tell Bixby **What is the square root of four?**

Note: As at the time of writing this guide, Bixby is unable to perform some simple mathematical conversions. For example, it is unable to convert meter to centimeter.

Using Bixby to Get Definitions

Note: As at the time of writing this guide, it appears that Bixby is unable to give meaning to words.

Bixby's Settings

The settings tab allows you to manage Bixby's functions. To access Bixby's settings:

1. Swipe in from the left edge of the screen while on the Home screen.

2. Tap the menu icon ⋮ located at top of the screen and tap **Settings**.

3. Tap an option.

The settings menu allows you to manage Bixby like a maven. I will advise that you take time to go through the various settings options on the settings page.

← Bixby settings page

How to Clear Bixby's Voice Interaction Data

To erase whatever voice interaction Bixby has stored:

4. Swipe in from the left edge of the screen while on the Home screen.

5. Tap the menu icon ⋮ located at the topmost part of the screen and tap **Settings**.

6. Scroll down and tap **Privacy**.

7. Tap **Delete Bixby Voice interaction data.**

Troubleshooting Bixby

Although much efforts have been put into making this virtual assistant, I am quite sure that Bixby will misbehave at one time or the other. When this happens, there are few things to do.

- **Ensure that you are connected to a strong network**: If you have a bad or no internet connection, Bixby may not work properly. Therefore, the first thing to check when Bixby starts to misbehave is the internet connection.

- **Use the Virtual Keyboard**: You may need to use the keyboard to pass your message to Bixby if you find out that it is not getting your speech. Many of what you say (If not all) can also be typed into the Bixby's search bar.

- **Try to Restart Your Phone**: If you find out that what I have mentioned above does not work, you may try restarting your phone because it may be that it is your phone that is confused and not Bixby.

Conclusion

Bixby is like a learning machine and it is being improved upon. If you are having difficulty passing your message across to it, you may try typing some of your commands into the command box. I strongly believe you will know how to use it more as time goes on. Don't forget that Rome was not built in a day.

Bixby Vision

Bixby allows you to interact with images in an educating manner. It also gives you more understanding of what you are looking at. When first using Bixby Vision, you may need to agree to some terms and conditions.

To Use Bixby Vision:
1. Launch the camera app of your phone.
2. Aim the lens of the camera at what you want to capture.
3. Tap the Bixby button and allow Bixby to examine the picture. You can use the Bixby Vision to extract texts, translate a language, scan Barcodes, shop etc.

Bixby vision button

4. Bixby will then display options based on what it thinks you are viewing. Choose an option. For example, if you are trying to extract a text, tap **Text** if this is among the options displayed.
5. To exit, tap the Bixby Vision again.

You can also access Bixby vision while using the Gallery app. Simply launch the **Gallery** app, tap an image and tap the Bixby button.

Hint: You can access the Bixby vision from the Air command screen, to do this, simply remove the S pen from your phone, tap the Bixby vision button and follow the onscreen instructions.

Using the Web

Internet App

Opening the Internet Browser

The first thing you will need to do to use the Internet app is to open it. This can be done by simply tapping on the **Internet** .

1. From the Home screen, tap **Internet**.

2. Alternatively, go to the app screen by swiping up from the bottom of the screen and tap **Samsung** folder. Tap **Internet** .

3. If you are using the Internet app for the first time, follow the prompts to get started.

Get to Know the Internet Browser Interface

When you open the Internet app, you should see the following buttons/icons:

| 1 | Favorite: **Tap this icon to bookmark a webpage.** |
| 2 | **Refresh:** Tapping this icon reloads a webpage. |

3	**Menu icon:** Tap this icon to access additional options such as **Find on page** and **save webpage** etc.
4	**Tabs:** Tap this to navigate between different webpages. Tap and hold the tab icon to quickly open your browser's home page.
5	**Bookmarks:** Tap this icon to access bookmark pages, saved pages and history.
6	**Home:** Tap this icon to go to the browser's home page. To quickly change the default Homepage, tap and hold the Home icon ⌂ and then select **Other.** Then enter the website of your choice (e.g. bing.com) and tap **OK**.
7	**Forward**: Tap this icon to return to the page you just left.
8	**Back:** Tap this icon to revisit the page you just visited. To quickly access browsing history, tap and hold the back button ‹
9	**Quick Menu:** Tap this button to access the quick menu. Quick menu allows you to quickly share a webpage, increase webpage font, or open a new tab. To move this icon to another location, simply tap, hold and drag

the icon to the new location. To remove the icon; tap, hold and drag it to the top of the screen (where ⊗ Remove icon is located).

Customizing the Home Page

The Home page is the page that opens when you open your Internet browser. Fortunately, you can choose what appears on your home page.

To do this:

- While the Internet browser is opened, tap menu icon ⋮ and then scroll down and tap on **Settings**.

207

- Tap **Home page** and then choose an option.

- To go to the Home page while using your internet browser, tap the internet browser Home button 🏠.

Tip: To quickly change the default Homepage, tap and hold the Home icon 🏠 and then select an option.

Using the Address/Search Bar

Every web browser must have an address bar and Internet browser also has one. This bar serves the function of URL address bar and search bar. By default, the searches done on this bar is executed by Google. To learn how to change the search engine to another one, please go to page 218.

You choose whether to launch a webpage or search for a term based on what you type into the address bar. For example, if you type **Windows Radar** into the address bar and tap **Go**, Google search results for that phrase is displayed. On the other hand, if you type **windowsradar.com** and tap **Go**, you will be taken to the website bearing the name.

Internet browser makes website suggestions to you based on the sites you have recently visited, to choose any of this suggested site, tap it.

When you begin to type inside the address bar, Internet browser automatically makes suggestions beneath your typing. You can choose any of these suggestions to make things faster.

Zooming a Webpage in Internet Browser

To zoom in a webpage in Internet browser, place two fingers on the webpage and spread them apart. To zoom out, place two fingers on the webpage and move them closer together. To force zoom a webpage that doesn't readily respond to a zoom request, turn on the **Manual zoom.** To do this, while the Internet browser is opened, tap menu icon ⋮ located at the top of the screen and then scroll down and tap on **Settings**. Tap the status switch next to **Manual Zoom.**

Using Tabs on Internet Browser

The tabs allow you to open different webpages at once. You can open many tabs at once on Internet browser.

To manage browsing tabs:

1. Tap the tab icon ⬚ located at the bottom of the screen.
2. To open a new tab, tap **New Tab**.

3. To access a tab you have opened before, tap the tab icon and then tap the desired tab.

4. To close a tab, tap the **X** icon at the top right corner of the thumbnail of the tab you want to close.
5. To close all tabs, while on the tabs' screen, tap **CLOSE ALL** located at the top of the screen.

Favorites (Bookmarks)

With several billions of webpages in the internet world, you just have to select your favorites. Just like other modern-day browsers, Internet browser gives you the opportunity to select a favorite or bookmark a page. This makes it easier to visit the website or webpage in the future.

To bookmark a webpage:

1. Open the website you want to bookmark.

2. Tap the menu icon ⋮ located at the top of the screen and then select **Add to Bookmarks**.

3. Key in the **Title** you want.

4. Tap **Save**.

Tip: To quickly add a bookmark, just open the webpage and tap ☆ next to the address bar.

Accessing Your Bookmarks/Favorites

After you have added a webpage to your favorites list, you will need to access this list sooner or later. To access your bookmarks, tap the Bookmark icon 📖 (located at the bottom of the screen).

Saving a Webpage

Webpages contain a lot of information and you will probably need to schedule some webpages for later reading. Saving a webpage is a great way to do this. When you find an interesting information online and you don't have the time to read it now, you can save it for a later reading.

To save a webpage, open the webpage and tap ⋮ (next to address bar) and then select **Save webpage**.

Accessing Your Saved Pages

After you have saved a page, you will need to access this page sooner or later. To do this, tap the **Bookmarks** icon (located at the bottom of the screen) and then tap **Saved Pages** located at the top of the screen.

Changing the Search Engine

The default search engine on Internet browser is Google. Some people may love to change this to another search engine.

You can change the Internet browser Search Engine by following the steps highlighted below:

1. While the browser is opened, tap menu icon ⋮ (next to address bar) and select **Settings**.

2. Tap on **Default search engine** and select a search engine.

Making Internet App Your Default Browser

If you have multiple browsers on your device, you can select internet app to be the default browser. To do this:

1. Swipe down from the top of the screen and select settings icon ✿ .

2. Tap **Apps** and then tap the menu icon ⋮ .
3. Tap **Default apps**.
4. Tap **Browser app** and choose **Samsung Internet**.

Hint: You can use the method mentioned above to set other favorite app(s) as default app(s). For example, if you have many email apps on your device, you can select a default email app using this method.

Managing the History List

If the secret mode is not enabled, Internet browser collects the history of the webpages you visit and stores it.

To access your history:

1. Tap the **Bookmarks** 📖 (located at the bottom of the screen).

2. Tap **History**.

Hint: To clear the browsing data, tap ⋮ > **Settings** > **Privacy** > **Delete personal data.** Select what you will like to delete and tap **Delete**.

Sharing a Webpage with Friends

To share your webpage with friends, open the Internet app and tap the menu icon ⋮ next to the address bar. Then tap on **Share**. Then choose an app and follow the prompts.

Add Your Favorite Webpage to the Home Screen

You can make your favorite webpage a shortcut on the Home screen. This allows you to easily access the webpage directly from your Home screen. To do this:

1. Open a webpage and tap on the menu icon ⋮ (next to the address bar).
2. Tap **Add shortcut on Home screen**.

220

Printing Web Pages on the Internet browser

Printing on the Internet browser is quite fantastic. You can initiate the printing process by tapping on the menu icon (the three dots icon next to the address bar). Then tap **Print.** Tap the **dropdown arrow** to select a printer. To adjust the printing options, tap **Copies**. To save the webpage as a pdf, select **Save as PDF** and then tap the yellow **PDF** icon to download.

Secret Mode

There are times when you will not want your browser to save any information about your visit to a webpage. For instance, if you don't want a website to save cookies on your device or you don't want your child to know you are browsing about favorite gifts to buy for them.

In addition, Secret mode browsing allows for multiple sessions. For example, you may access your Yahoo mail account (or another web account) on a normal window and use the Secret mode tab to open the Yahoo mail account of that of your friend or family member without logging out of your own account. Pages viewed in secret mode are not listed in your browser history or search history, and leave no traces (such as cookies) on your device.

To activate the Secret mode, in the toolbar at the bottom of the screen, tap **Tabs** → **Turn on Secret mode.**

Then tap **Set password** to protect your Secret mode data with a password. You may also tap **Do not use password** if you don't want to use a password.

To deactivate the Secret mode, close the Internet app or tap the tab button and then select **Turn Off Secret Mode.**

More on Internet browser Settings

Many options under settings have already been discussed, but there are still some that I will like to mention.

1. **Auto fill profile:** Use this option to enable Internet browser to save your form entries whenever you fill in information into an online form so that it can be used when you are filling similar forms in the future.

2. **Privacy**: Use this option to access settings such as **cookies**, **personal data** and so on. You can use the privacy tab to delete history information on your browser. To do this, tap **Delete personal data**.

3. **Advanced**: Use this option to access advanced options like **JavaScript**, **Pop-up blocker**, **Status bar**, **Manage website data** and **Receive web notifications**.

4. **About Samsung Internet:** Use this option to get software information about the Internet app.

More on the Menu Icon

Many options under the **menu** tab ⋮ have already been discussed, but I will still like to point out few more things.

1. **Add to Quick access**: Use this option to add a webpage to your quick access list so that you can access it easily in the future.

2. **Add shortcut on Home screen:** Use this option to make a webpage a shortcut on your Home screen.

3. **Find on page:** Use this option to search for a word or a phrase on a webpage.

4. **Request desktop site:** Use this option to request the desktop version of a webpage.

Troubleshooting the Internet browser

Internet browser may sometimes refuse to work properly, or it may hang. If this happens, just close the browser and open it again. To close the Internet app, tap the recent button to view all the opened apps and then tap **X** next to the Internet app thumbnail. If the browser refuses to close, try restarting your phone.

Troubleshooting Internet Connection when Using the Internet Browser

Internet browser may sometimes refuse to browse the internet. When this happens, you may try any of the suggestions below:

1. Check if you are connected to a wireless network. When Wi-Fi is connected, active, and it is communicating with a wireless Access Point, **Wi-Fi active icon** is displayed on the status bar at the top of the screen. If your phone is not connected to a network, swipe down from the top of the screen and tap **settings icon** > **Connections**. Tap **Wi-Fi**, and then tap On/Off to turn Wi-Fi on.

Wi-Fi Active Icon

2. If you are trying to use a cellular connection and not a Wi-Fi connection, then check your cellular data connection. Swipe down from the top of the screen, tap the **settings icon** > **Connections** > **Data Usage**. Then make sure the switch next to **Mobile data** is turned on.

3. If you are trying to roam while abroad, check that you have allowed roaming. Swipe down from the top of the screen and tap the **settings icon** ⚙ **> Connections > Mobile networks > Data Roaming**. Then make sure the switch next to **Data Roaming** is switched on. Please note that when roaming, international roaming charges may apply.

If after trying all the options above, and you can't still browse, then make sure that you have not mistakenly/knowingly installed a new browsing setting on your phone. If you have installed new settings from a text message, then uninstall the new settings. To do this, swipe down from the top of the screen and tap the **settings icon** ⚙ **> Apps**. Look for the new settings. Tap the new settings and tap **Uninstall**.

Communication

Calling

Learn how to use the calling functions, such as making and answering calls, using options available during a call, and using call-related features.

Making, Answering, Rejecting and Silencing a Call

To make a call or silence a call:

1. While on the home screen, tap **Phone** and enter a phone number. If the keypad does not appear on the screen, tap the keypad button to show the keypad. To call a number on your contact, tap the **Contact** button on the Phone app screen.

227

2. To make a call from the **Recents** tab, tap the **Recents** tab located at the top of the screen.

3. To make a phone call, tap a contact and then tap the phone icon .

[Screenshot showing a contacts list with "Example" contact selected, with arrows indicating "Tap the contact you want to call" and "Call icon"]

4. To silence or reduce the volume of an incoming call, press the volume down button.

Hint: You can access apps/items on your phone while receiving a call. To do this, tap the home key ⬜ located at the lower side of the screen and tap the item/app you want to access.

To answer a call or reject an incoming call:

1. To receive an incoming call, tap or drag the **Green phone icon** 📞.

2. To decline an incoming call, tap or drag the **Red phone icon** 📞.

229

3. To reply with a text, swipe up from the bottom of the screen and then tap one of the pre-written messages. Alternatively, tap **Compose new message**, and write your message.

Hint: If you are using an app, a pop-up screen is displayed for the incoming call, just tap the corresponding icon to accept, decline the call or reply with a message.

In addition, you can create rejection messages of your own. From the Home screen, tap **Phone > Menu icon ⋮ > Settings > Quick decline message** , enter a message, and then tap **Plus icon +.**

If a phone number calls you and you don't have it in your contact, you can easily add it to you contact. To do this, tap **Phone** app and tap **Recents.** Then tap the contact and tap **Details.** Tap **Create Contact** and follow the prompts.

Tip: To quickly reject an incoming call with a preset rejection message, place your finger on the heart rate monitor for two seconds while the phone screen is facing down. The heart rate monitor is located under the flash light at the back of your phone. *Please note that this option only works when your device is turned over and the screen is off.*

You can edit the preset rejection message. To do this:

1. Swipe down from the top of the screen and select settings icon . Tap **Display** tab.
2. Scroll down and tap **Edge Screen**.
3. Tap **Edge Lighting**.
4. Tap the menu icon located at the top of the screen.

231

5. Tap **Quick reply**.
6. Type in a **Quick Reply Message** and tap the back icon next to QUICK REPLY to save the changes.

Tap this icon to save changes

QUICK REPLY

When the screen is off and the phone is turned face down, incoming calls will show on Edge lighting. Decline an incoming call and send a preset message to the caller by placing your finger on the heart rate sensor for 2 seconds.

QUICK REPLY MESSAGE
Kindly call back later.

Learn How to Use Your Phone During a Call

You can perform any of these tasks when on a call:

Number	Function
1.	Tap the **Menu icon** to hold a current call, view a contact or add a number to contact, or send a message.
2.	Tap the Bluetooth icon to connect to a Bluetooth headset while on a call.

233

3.	Tap this icon to mute the microphone.
4.	Tap the red phone icon to **end a call**.
5.	Tap the keypad icon to access the keypad. To hide the keypad, tap the **Hide** icon.
6.	To turn Speakerphone on or off, tap the speaker icon.
7.	Tap the plus icon to add another contact to a call or start another call.
8.	Tap extra volume icon to add extra volume to a call.

Tip: To access the application screen while on a call, tap the Home button. If you want to return to the call screen, swipe down from the top of the screen and tap the current call.

Place a New Call While on a Call (Conference Calling)

If your network service provider supports this feature, you can make another call while a call is in progress.

1. From the active call screen, tap + **Add call**.

2. Dial the new number and tap 📞 **Dial**. When the call is answered:

    i. Tap ⟲ **Swap** to switch between the two calls.

    ii. Tap ⤳ **Merge** to turn the call to a conference call.

234

3. To end a call while on a conference call mode, tap the dropdown arrow (next to **Conference call**) and then select **Drop** next to the call you want to end.

Emergency Calling

You can use Samsung Galaxy Note 8 to make an emergency call. From the Home screen, tap **Phone** icon and enter the emergency telephone number. Note that if you dial 911 in the U.S, your location details may be provided to an emergency service provider even if your settings does not support this.
Please note that an emergency number can be dialed even if the phone is locked.

Using Call Waiting

Call waiting allows you to get another call while you're already in one.

1. To answer the new call, drag 📞 **Answer** to the right direction and then choose an option:
    i. **Put ...on hold** to place the previous caller on hold while you answer the new call.
    ii. **Merge with...** to add the new caller to the current call.
    iii. **End call with...** to end the previous call and answer the new call.
2. Once the other call is answered, tap the 🔄 swap icon next to the contact or number you wish to continue talking to. The other(s) will be put on hold.

Please note that call waiting may be disabled by default. To enable this feature, tap **Phone** > **Menu icon** ⋮ > **Settings** > **More settings,** and then tap the switch next to **Call waiting.**

Using the Speed Dial Options

The speed dial allows you to quickly access a number in your contact. To set up speed dial:

236

1. Tap the phone icon
2. Tap **Contacts** located at the top of the screen.
3. Tap **menu icon** located at the top of the screen.
4. Tap **Speed dial**.
5. To add a contact to the speed dial, tap the contact icon to add a contact.
6. To change the speed dial number, tap the dropdown arrow and pick a number. Number one is reserved for voicemail.

SPEED DIAL

Assign contacts

Dropdown arrow

1 — Voicemail

2 — Example 2 — 0813 2

7. To call a contact you have added, tap the phone app icon and from the dial pad, press and hold the number assigned to the desired contact. To call a contact assigned to

a two-digit speed dial, dial the first number, then press and hold the 2nd number.

8. To delete a speed dial number, tap the **Minus (-)** icon next to the assigned contact. Removing a contact from a speed dial list will not delete it from your phone.

Using the Fixed Dialing Option

If you want to select the numbers your mobile phone can call, you need to turn on the fixed dialing. Once done, you can only call the selected numbers and emergency numbers.

1. From the Home screen, tap **PHONE app icon**.
2. Tap **menu icon** located at the top of the screen.
3. Tap **Settings**.
4. Scroll down and tap **More settings**.
5. Tap **Fixed Dialing Numbers**.
6. To turn the fixed dialing on, tap **Turn on FDN**, type in your **PIN2** and tap **OK**. Please contact your local network service provider for your PIN2.
7. To turn the fixed dialing off, tap **Turn off FDN**, enter your **PIN2** and tap OK. Please contact your local network service provider for your PIN2.

Note: I am not sure if all network providers support this feature. If you notice that this feature is not available on your phone, you may need to contact your service provider to know if you can use this feature.

Adding Fixed Dialing Numbers

1. Repeat the steps 1 to 5 above.
2. Tap **FDN List**.
3. Tap **ADD** located at the top of the screen.
4. Tap **Name** and enter the required name.
5. Tap **NUMBER** and enter the required phone number.
6. Tap **PIN2** and enter the PIN2. Please contact your local network service provider for your PIN2.
7. Tap **SAVE** located at the top of the screen.

Please note that when FDN is enabled, you may not be able to call any other numbers, apart from the numbers on the FDN list and the emergency numbers.

Call Forwarding (Diverting Calls to Another Number)

When you are busy, you can forward incoming calls to another phone number. Please note that your network provider will need to support this feature for it to be available.

1. From the Home screen, tap **PHONE app icon**.
2. Tap **menu icon** located at the top of the screen.

239

3. Tap **Settings**.
4. Scroll down and tap **More settings**.
5. Tap **Call forwarding**.
6. Tap the required divert type and follow the onscreen instructions. For example, to forward all your calls, tap **Always forward**.
7. To turn off call forwarding, select a divert type and select **turn off/disable.**

Note: Please note that when the call forwarding option is enable, you should see the call forwarding icon (see the picture below) on the notification bar at the top of the screen.

In addition, depending on your network provider, you may be able to forward calls to your voice mail and listen to them later.

Block Calls

If your service provider supports this feature, you may be able to avoid receiving calls from certain numbers. However, please note that turning call blocking on does not block text messages. If you want to know how to block text messages, please go to page 247. In addition, the call blocking feature may not affect phone calls made or received via apps (e.g. Skype) installed on your device.
Please note that features available under Call blocking may differ from one service provider to another.

1. From the Home screen, tap **PHONE app icon**.
2. Tap **menu icon** located at the top of the screen.
3. Tap **Settings**.
4. Tap **Block numbers**.
5. To add a number to your block list, enter the desired phone number in the **Add phone number** field, then tap the + icon.

   To go into your contacts, tap Contacts icon.
6. To remove a number from your block list, tap the Minus (-) icon next to a name or number on your block list.
7. To make sure that only the numbers that you have their contacts can call you, tap the status switch next to **Block unknown callers**.

Note: In certain instances, blocking anonymous call may be unbeneficial and even dangerous. For example, blocking anonymous call may prevent you from accepting calls from those who have something important to tell you (unless you have their contacts).

What about Caller ID

If your service provider supports this feature, you may prevent your service provider from displaying your number(ID) when you call another person.

1. From the Home screen, tap **PHONE app icon** .
2. Tap **menu icon** located at the top of the screen.
3. Tap **Settings**.
4. Scroll down and tap **More settings**.

5. Tap **Show my caller ID** and then choose an option.

Using the Messaging app

This app allows you to send texts, images, and video messages to other SMS and MMS devices.

To start or manage a conversation:

1. Tap the **Messages** app icon from Home screen.

243

2. Tap the new message icon located at the bottom right corner of the screen.
3. Type in the first letters of the recipient's name. Your list filters as you type. Then tap the required contact. Note, depending on your service provider, you can add up to 20 contacts (if not more). If you don't have the number in your contact, just key in the number in **Search Contacts or enter number field**. To remove a contact from the send list, just tap the minus icon (-) next to the contact.
4. Tap the **Compose** icon located at the top of the screen and write the text for your SMS/MMS.

5. To attach a file such as audio, tap the Paper clip icon and follow the prompts.

Tap this icon to attach a file

Choose from these three options and then choose the file you want to attach

6. When you are done, tap **Send**.
7. To reply a message, tap the message and then enter a message in the reply field. Tap **Send** when you are done.
8. To **Delete** a conversation, press and hold the message in question and tap on **Delete.**
9. In a conversation, you can press and hold a message to **forward, copy, share** or **delete** the message.

Message Options ← Message Options

(Menu shown: Message options — Delete, Send to Reminder, Copy text, Forward, Share, Lock)

Hints:

- If you receive an attachment, you can tap on the attachment to view it. To save an attachment, tap and hold the attachment and select **save attachment**. You can also tap the **Share** icon to share the attachment. To view saved attachments, go to the app screen and tap **Samsung** folder and then tap **My files.** Alternatively, visit **Photos/Gallery** app if the attachment is an image.

- To customize your message settings, from the message screen, tap menu icon ⋮ and select **Settings.** Tap the desired setting to adjust. To access more settings, tap **More Settings.** For example, to change the message background, tap **Backgrounds** and choose a background. *Please note that the features available on message settings may differ from one service provider to another.*

246

Message settings menu

- **You can block text messages** from certain numbers, if your service provider supports this feature. To do this, Tap the menu icon ⋮ > **Settings** > **Block messages** > **Block numbers**. Then enter the desired number in the **Phone number** field and tap the + icon to add the entered number to the message block list. To go into your contacts/ message inbox, tap **Contacts/Inbox**. To remove a number from the message block list, tap the minus (-) icon.

Please note that turning the text blocking option on does not block calls. If you want to know how to block calls, please go to page 241.

EMAIL APP

Introduction

Samsung Galaxy Note 8 always comes preloaded with an email app for sending and receiving emails. One of the things you will need to do when you start using your device is to set up an email account. In this section of the guide, I will be discussing how to use your mail app like a maven.

How to Add Your Email Accounts to the Email app

You probably have many email accounts and you may wish to add these accounts to the email app on your device.

The email accounts you can add to the Mail app include Google Mail, Yahoo Mail, iCloud, Exchange, Outlook among others.

To add an email account:

- Swipe down from the top of the screen and select settings icon ⚙.

- Tap **Cloud and accounts**.

- Tap **Account.**

- Tap **Add account.**

- Select the required account. For example, to add a Gmail account, tap **Google** and follow the on-screen instructions. To add another email account, tap **Email**. Enter the desired **Email address**, the **Password**, and tap **SIGN IN**. Then follow the prompts to complete the setup.

Special Note on Adding Exchange Account to the Email App

Following the instructions above might not be enough when you want to add your Exchange account to the Email app and you may need an extra information. You may need to obtain from your Exchange administrator or provider the account's server address, domain name, and username in addition to your email address and password.

How to Compose and Send an Email Message Using the Email App

You can easily send an email message to your friends or organization using the Email App. In this section of the guide, we will be exploring how to compose and send an email message.

To send an email message:

- To send or receive an email, from the Home screen, swipe up and tap **Email** . If you can't see the Email app, check **Samsung** folder on the application screen.

- To change to another email account if multiple email accounts are configured, swipe right from the left edge of the screen and tap an account.

- To compose a new email, tap the new email icon located at the bottom of the screen.

- Tap the field next to **To** and type in the email address of the recipient. You can also tap the contact icon to view your contacts.

- To send a copy to another person, tap the dropdown icon next to **To** and type the person's email address in the **Cc/Bcc** field.

Tip: Cc means Carbon Copy. If you use the Cc option to send a message to many recipients, all the recipients will see the message and all other email addresses that have received the message. On the other hand, Bcc stands for Blind Carbon Copy. If you use Bcc option to send a message to many recipients, all the recipients will see the message, but will not see other email addresses that have received the message.

- Tap **Subject** field and key in the subject of your email.
- Tap the text input field and write the text for your email.
- You can use the tab at the bottom of the screen to perform the following actions:

252

1. **Pen:** This option allows you to write message with the S Pen.

2. **Undo:** Tap to undo an action.

3. **Redo:** Tap to redo an action.

4. **Image:** Tap this to add an image.

5. **Font:** Tap this to change the font type.

6. **Font Size**: Use this option to change the font size of your text.

7. **Bold**: You can bold a part or your entire message using this feature. To bold a text, select the text(s) and tap the **B** icon.

8. **Italicize**: You can make your text appear italicized by clicking on the *I* icon.

9. **Underline**: Use the U icon to underline a text.

10. **Font color**: Tap this to change the font color.

11. **Font background color**: Tap this to change the font background color.

12. **Numbering**: Tap this to create a numbered list.

13. **Bullets:** Tap this to create a bullet list.

14. **Increase indent**: Tap this to move the paragraph farther away from the margin.

To access more formatting options, swipe the formatting icons to the left or right. (See the arrows below).

- When you are satisfied with the message and you are ready to send it, tap **Send** located at the top of the Email app screen.

Note: Before you can apply some of the formatting options above to a block of texts, you will need to select the texts. To do this, tap and hold a word, and then drag ⬤ or ⬤ to select the texts you want.

Attaching a file

You can insert an attachment into your message by clicking on **ATTACH** located at the top of the screen. Select whether your attachment is a **DOCUMENT,** a **GALLERY,** or **OTHER (e.g. audio file).** Locate and tap on the file you want to attach.

To view saved attachments, go to app screen and tap **Samsung** folder. Then tap **My files.** Alternatively, visit **Photos/Gallery** app if the attachment is an image.

Managing a Received Email

One of the most important functions of any email app is the ability to receive incoming messages. By default, Email app searches for new messages and alerts you when there is one.

New messages are either stored in Inbox or Junk/Trash/Spam folder and these are the two places to check if you are expecting an email.

To see if there is a new message, swipe down from the top of the screen.

To read a message:

- Tap on the subject of a message to open the message text in the preview pane.

- Those messages that you have not yet read should appear bold.

- The attachment icon means that a message has an attachment.

- The Email app allows you to perform the following actions on a message in your inbox:

| Reply | Reply all | Forward | Delete | Thread |

If the icons above are not showing up while viewing an email message, swipe down/up from the middle of the screen.

- **Reply:** Tap this button to reply an email message. When you tap this button, a new window appears. This window is similar to what appears when you tap on a new email button but with a slight difference. The reply window contains the recipient's name and the subject. In addition, the original message usually appears at the bottom of your reply for reference.

- **Reply All:** If the message in your inbox is addressed to several people, you can choose to reply all those people by tapping **Reply All.** You can know whether an email is sent to many people by tapping **Details** tab next to the sender's name/address.

- **Forward:** Use this option to send a copy of an email in your inbox to your friends or associates. When you tap on the **Forward** button, a message window with a subject line preceded by "FW:" appears. The original message address (To and From), date, subject, attachment, and text are also included. In addition, you will have the option to fill in the email address of the person to whom you are sending the message.

- **Delete:** Use this option to delete a message from your inbox. Alternatively, tap and hold the email and select **Delete.**

Hint: When you open the Email app inbox to check a mail, the name of the sender is usually displayed on the top of the message pane. To see the email address of whoever sent the message, tap the mail and then tap **DETAILS** next to sender's name/address.

How to Open and Save an Attachment in the Email App

The email with an attachment will have a paper clip icon displayed next to the address of the sender when you check your message inbox.

To open an attachment:

1. Tap the message that has the attachment, as indicated by a paper clip icon.

2. When the message opens, tap the attachment that you want to open and tap **SAVE**. If your device is not having an appropriate program to open the attachment, you may be unable to view the attachment. In a situation like this, you will need to install the appropriate program for the type of file. You may ask the person that sent the message about which program to use to open the attachment.

3. To view saved attachments, go to app screen and tap **Samsung** folder. Tap **My files** and then tap **Downloads.** Alternatively, if the attachment is an image, go to **Photos/Gallery** app.

Managing the Settings Options

Some of the options under Email Settings have already been discussed. But I will still like to briefly mention some few more things.

- To access the Email app settings, Open the Email app and tap ☰ located at the left top corner of the screen.

```
                         ✱ ✻ 📶 100% 🔋 15:30
☰  INBOX
   pharmibrahimguides@gmail.co..    EDIT    SORT BY

   Microsoft Office 365              May 17
   Getting Started: Welcome to Office 365
   Welcome to Office 365 This is the first email i...    ☆
```

- Tap on **Settings** ⚙ located at the top of the screen.

- Under **General** tab, tap an option. To configure specific settings for an account, tap the account.
- To delete an account from your device, tap the email account and then tap **REMOVE** next to the account name.

How to Remove the Default Email Signature in the Email App

You can use the Signature tab to command the Email app what signature to include in a message. To do this, open the email app, tap ☰ and then tap **Settings** ⚙. Tap the desired account, tap **Signature**, and then key in a signature of your choice. Tap **DONE** located at the top of the screen. You can use the switch next to Signature to enable or disable this feature.

Note: An email signature is a text that appears by default after the body of your message. You may set your email signature to be your name or your brand.

Personal Information

Contacts

This app allows you to create and manage a list of your personal or business contacts. You can save names, mobile phone numbers, home phone numbers, email addresses, and more.

To create a contact:

1. While on the Home screen, swipe up and tap on **Contact** app.

2. Tap on **Add contact** icon located at the lower right corner of the screen.

3. Select where you want to save the contact by tapping the address book drop down list. See the picture below.

4. Fill in the details by tapping on each item on the screen.

5. To assign a contact to a group, tap **Group.**
6. To access more options, tap on **View more**.

7. When you are done, tap **Save** located at the top of the screen.

Hint: To search for a contact, open the contact app and tap the **search** bar (located at the top of the screen), and start typing a name. The list filters as you write.

When you receive a message, you can easily save the number if it is not yet saved in your contacts. To do this, tap the messaging app.

Tap a conversation, tap the menu icon located at the top right corner of the screen and select **Add to contacts**. Then tap **Create Contact** (located at the bottom of the screen). Follow the on-screen instructions to finish the process.

To manage a contact:

1. From the app screen, tap on the **Contact** app.
2. Tap on a contact from the list.
3. Tap the **details** icon (the last icon on the left).

4. Tap **EDIT** located at the top of the screen and then enter the new details.

5. To delete a contact, open the contact app, tap and hold the contact you want to delete and then tap on **Delete** located at the top of the screen. You can also use the method to delete many contacts at once. All you have to do is to select all the contacts you want to delete and then tap **Delete**.
6. To share a contact, tap and hold the contact you want to share and then tap **Share.**

To link a contact, tap the contact, tap **Details** and then tap the menu icon .

Tap **Link contacts** or **Merge contacts** and tap the contacts to link with. Tap **Link**. Linking two contacts is important if you have separate entries for the same contact from different social networking services or email accounts.

To unlink a contact, tap the contact you want to unlink, tap **Details** and then tap the menu icon . Tap **Managed Link contacts** and tap the minus icon (--) beside the contact you want to unlink. To link another contact, tap **Link Another Contact**.

Copy contacts

If you have some contacts stored on your SIM card, you can copy them to your phone with some simple steps.

1. From the app screen, tap on the **Contact** app.
2. Tap the menu icon .
3. Tap **Manage contacts**.
4. Tap **Import/Export contacts**.

5. Tap **Import**.
6. Select where you are copying the contacts from.
7. If you want to import all the contacts, tap **ALL** located at the top of the screen.
8. Tap **DONE**.
9. Tap **Phone** or where you are sending the contacts to.
10. Tap **Import.**

Tip: You can **export** contacts from your phone to other places by following the steps similar to the ones mentioned above. But don't forget that you will select **Export** (and not Import).

Contact Group

If you will like to send a message to several people at the same time, I will advise that you create a contact group. You can create a contact group for friends and family members in order to reach them easily.

To create a group:

1. From the app screen, tap on the **Contact** app.
2. Tap the menu icon .
3. Tap on **Groups** and tap **Create**.

4. Fill in the name for the group and tap **Add member** to add members to the newly created group.
5. Tap **Save**.

To add members to a group:

1. From the app screen, tap on **Contact** app.
2. Tap menu icon .
3. Tap on **GROUPS** and tap a group.
4. Tap **Edit**.

5. Tap **Add Member**. Then tap on a contact to add and tap **Done**.
6. Tap **Save** to save the changes.

Tip: To remove a contact from a group follow steps 1 to 4 above and then tap **Delete** (the minus icon) next to the contact you want to remove.

Managing a group contact:

1. From the app screen, tap on the **Contact** app.
2. Tap the menu icon .
3. Tap on **GROUPS** and tap a group.

4. To send a message to a group, tap **Menu icon** ⋮ and tap **Send message**.

5. To send an email to a group, tap **Menu icon** ⋮ and tap **Send email**.

Deleting a group:

1. From the app screen, tap on the **Contact** app.
2. Tap the menu icon ⋮ .
3. Tap on **GROUPS** and tap a group.
4. Tap **Menu icon** ⋮ .
5. Tap **Delete**.
6. Tap **Group only** to delete only the group. Tap **Group and members** to delete both the group and the contacts in the group.

Hint: To customize the Contact app, tap on the **Contact** app, tap the **Menu icon** ⋮ and then tap **Settings**.

272

< CONTACTS SETTINGS

Profile sharing

DISPLAY

Contacts to display
All contacts

Sort by
First name

Name format
First, last

Show Frequently contacted

MORE SETTINGS

Share multiple contacts
As one file

About Contacts

Use these settings options to customize the contact app

Accessibility Features – the Special Features for Easy Usage

Accessibility services are special features for those with physical challenges. In addition, it also provides you the opportunity to control your phone in a special way.

Vision

This option allows you to hear what is happening on the screen as you touch/interact with the phone screen.

To use the vision settings:
1. Swipe down from the top of the screen and select the settings icon ⚙.
2. Scroll down and tap **Accessibility**.
3. Tap **Vision**.
4. Tap the desired option. Interestingly, for complex options, usually, there are explanations beneath them. You can read these explanations to get what each option represents.

Hint: Vision tab contains those settings that help with vision. These settings are particularly good for visually impaired person.

Hearing

This tab allows you to control sound related settings. For example, you can turn off all sounds using this feature.

To use the Hearing settings:

1. Swipe down from the top of the screen and select the settings icon ⚙.
2. Scroll down and tap **Accessibility.**
3. Tap **Hearing.**
4. Tap the desired option. Interestingly, for complex options, usually, there are explanations beneath them. You can read these explanations to get what each option represents.

Hint: The settings under the hearing tab is particularly good for hearing impaired person. For example, if you are using hearing aid, you can see the settings for your hearing aid under this tab.

In addition, you can turn on the flash notification if you want your phone to flash light when there is a notification.

> **FLASH NOTIFICATION**
>
> Flash the camera light or the screen when you receive notifications or when alarms sound.
>
> Camera light
>
> Screen

Dexterity and Interaction

This option allows you to control your device in a special way. For example, you can control your device with your customized switches using the **Universal switches** tab. Although, I will advise you don't tamper with the **Universal switches** unless you know much about it. If you mistakenly switch on **Universal switches** and you wish to turn it off, just press the power button and the volume up button together once.

To use Dexterity and interaction:
1. Swipe down from the top of the screen and select the settings icon ✿.
2. Scroll down and tap **Accessibility**.
3. Tap **Dexterity and interaction**.

4. Tap the desired option. Interestingly, for complex options, usually, there are explanations beneath them. You can read these explanations to get what each option represents.

Hint: Dexterity and interaction tab contains those settings that help you to control your device with gestures.

More settings

This option allows you to access some extra accessibility settings. For example, you can export your accessibility settings and share them with another device using the settings (**Accessibility settings backup**) under this tab.

Services

This tab allows you to access additional accessibility app(s).

TOOLS

Easy Mode

Easy mode provides a simpler layout and bigger icons on the Home screen, thereby enhancing visual experience and easier use. Unfortunately, not all app features are available in Easy mode.

To enable and manage Easy mode:
1. Swipe down from the top of the screen and select settings icon ⚙. Tap **Display** tab.
2. Tap **Easy mode**.
3. Tap **Easy mode** to enable this feature.
4. If available, use the switch next to each app to add or remove.
5. Tap **Apply** located at the top of the screen to save your settings. Then tap the Home key to return to the Home screen.
6. When Easy mode is enabled, you can add a shortcut to your favorite contacts. To add a shortcut to a contact; from the Home screen, swipe the screen to the right. Then tap the plus icon.

Tap this icon to add a contact to the home screen

To disable Easy mode:

1. Swipe down from the top of the screen and select settings icon . Tap **Display** tab.
2. Tap **Easy mode**.
3. Tap **Standard mode** to exit Easy mode.
4. Tap **Apply** to effect the changes.

Do Not Disturb

Do not disturb gives you the opportunity to prevent unnecessary disturbances from your phone. To quickly access this feature and customize it, swipe down from the top of the screen using two fingers and then tap and hold **Do Not disturb** for two or three seconds. Please note that you may need to swipe to the right to access more quick settings options before you can see the **Do Not disturb** icon.

Then select an option.

If you choose to schedule Do Not Disturb, then use **Days, Start time** and **End time** to customize your experience.

≡ ≡ ≡ ≡ * ⁂ 100% 🔋 21:04

< **DO NOT DISTURB**

Set your device to mute all calls, alerts, and
media, except for your selected exceptions.

Turn on now

Turn on as scheduled
Turn Do not disturb on and off automatically
at scheduled times.

Days
Mon,Tue,Wed,Thu,Fri,Sat,Sun

Start time
22:00

End time
07:00 next day

Allow exceptions
Alarms only

Hide visual notifications
Off

If you are scheduling "Do Not Disturb" then use these three options to customize it.

283

Creating Schedules and More with the Calendar App

Your phone provides you with a **calendar** app to help you organize your schedules and tasks more conveniently and effectively. You can create schedules and add events.

➢ **To create an event:**

1. From the Home screen, swipe up and tap on **Calendar**.

2. Tap the plus icon at the lower right side of the screen and enter the details.

3. To set the start and the end date of the event, tap **Start/End**.

284

4. When you are done, tap **Save** (located at the top of the screen).

Hint: Your phone will give you a notification when the time for an event arrives.

➢ **To view an event/schedule:**

1. From the Home screen, swipe up and tap on **Calendar**.
2. To change the calendar view, tap **View** (located at the top of the screen).
3. Tap the desired view.
4. Then tap on an event to view.

➢ **To edit, share or delete an event:**

285

1. From the Home screen, swipe up and tap on **Calendar**.
2. To change the calendar view, tap **View** (located at the top of the screen). Tap the desired view.
3. Then tap on an event to view.
4. To delete an event, tap and hold the event and select **Delete**.
5. To share an event, tap and hold the event and select **Share**.
6. To edit an event, tap and hold the event and select **Edit**.

> **To change your calendar view**

1. From the Home screen, swipe up and tap on **Calendar.**
2. To change the calendar view, tap **View** (located at the top of the screen). Tap the desired view.

286

Hint: To customize the calendar app, from the Home screen, swipe up and tap **Calendar** . Tap the menu icon at the top of the screen. Tap **settings** and choose an option.

Using the Camera

Samsung Galaxy Note 8 comes with two rear-facing cameras, a front-facing camera and an LED flash. With these cameras, you can capture an image or record a video.

Note: The memory capacity of the images taken may differ depending on the settings, shooting scenes and shooting conditions.

Number	Function
1.	Front-facing/rear-facing camera switch
2.	Expand View/Full View
3.	LED Flash button
4.	Camera settings
5.	Stickers
6.	Preview thumbnail tab
7.	Camera button
8.	Video button
9.	Live Focus. This option allows you to have a clearer picture of an object.
10.	Bixby Vision button. Tap this icon to get more information about the picture you are viewing. To learn more about Bixby vision, please see page 202.
11.	Zoom button

➤ To Capture a photo

1. While the phone is locked, double-press the Power Key (at the side of the phone) to launch the camera app. Please note that you may need to enable this feature. To do this, please go to page 291. Alternatively, from the app screen, tap **Camera.**

2. Aim the lens at the subject and make any necessary adjustments. To focus any part of the screen, tap that part of the screen.

3. To adjust the picture size, tap settings ⚙ and then tap the **Picture size**. Please note that the picture size you pick may affect the memory size of your captured image.

4 Tap **front-facing/rear-facing icon** to switch between the front-facing and rear-facing cameras.

5. To zoom in, place two fingers on the screen and spread them apart. Do the reverse to zoom out.

6. To turn geotagging on or off, tap the settings icon ⚙. Scroll down and tap the indicator next to "LOCATION TAGS" to turn the function on or off. Then tap OK. Geotagging allows you to attach a GPS location tag to an image.

7. Tap on **camera button** when you are done adjusting the settings.

Note: You can choose to enable or disable **Review pictures**. To disable **Review pictures,** tap the settings icon ✿ while on the camera app and tap the switch next to **Review pictures**. When the image review is enabled, you will see a preview of each photo immediately after you take a picture. This allows you to immediately delete the picture if you are not satisfied with it.

Tip: To change the picture storage location to SD card, while on the camera app screen, tap the settings icon ✿ and then scroll down and tap **Storage Location.** Then select **SD card** from the option that appears.

To open the Camera by quickly pressing the Power key twice:

1. Swipe down from the top of the screen and select the settings icon ✿ .

2. Tap **Advanced features.**

3. Tap **Quick launch camera** and tap the switch to activate it.

To customize camera settings:

1. When the phone is locked, double-press the Power Key (at the side of the phone) to launch the camera app. Please note that you may need to enable this feature. To do this, see above. Alternatively, from the Home screen, tap **Camera.**

2. Tap the settings icon ✿ .

3. Adjust the various settings as you like.

Hint: Camera settings consist of a lot of features, and you may not need to touch some of these features. In fact, the default settings are enough for many users.

If someone adjusts the camera settings the way you don't like and you wish to restore the camera settings to factory settings, follow these steps. Tap the settings icon ⚙ while on the camera app screen, scroll down and tap **Reset settings.** Tap **Reset** when prompted.

Recording a video

1. When the phone is locked, double-press the Power Key (at the side of the phone) to launch the camera app. Please note that you may need to enable this feature. To do this, see page 291. Alternatively, from the Home screen, tap **Camera.**

2 Tap on the video button to start recording.

3. To zoom in while recording, place two fingers on the screen and spread them apart. To zoom out, move the two fingers closer together.

4. When done with the recording, tap the **video button** again.

6. To view your recorded videos, go to **Gallery/Photos** app.

More about "MODES" in Camera app

Please note that some modes may not be available when using the front/rear camera. To access camera modes, swipe right on the camera app screen to change from camera to different shooting modes.

Pro: This feature allows you to manually adjust settings like color tone and white balance. I will advise you to leave this option if you are a newbie. The default settings might just be enough for you.

Virtual shot: Create multi-directional views of objects.

Panorama: This feature allows you to capture picture with elongated field of view. For example, you will find this feature important when trying to take the picture of a waterfall because of the large field of view. The panorama feature present on Samsung Galaxy Note 8 can be used to create an extended horizontal or vertical image.

Slow motion: This allows you to record a video for viewing it in a slow motion. You have the option to specify sections of your videos to be played in a slow motion.

Food: Use this option to take a detailed picture of food.

Hyperlapse: This option allows you to record scenes, such as passing cars, and view them as fast-motion videos.

Editing Your Photos

You can use your phone to edit photos.

1. Swipe up the screen while on the Home screen, and tap on **Gallery/Photos**.

2. Tap on the photo you want to edit.

3. Then tap the **Edit icon** and then pick any editing tool(s).

Connectivity

PC Connections

Your phone can be connected to a PC with a USB cable. This will enable you to transfer files such as audio files, document files and image files to your phone from your PC.

Warning: Do not disconnect the USB cable from a computer while the device is transferring or accessing data. This may result in data loss or damage to your phone.

Transferring content via USB

1. Connect your device to a PC with an appropriate USB cable (like the one that came with your phone).
2. When prompted to allow an access to phone data, tap **Allow.** If you don't choose Allow, your PC may not see your phone.

3. Slide down from the top of the screen and tap the USB option **(USB for file transfer)**.

4. Tap **Transfer Files**.

5. Your Samsung Galaxy Note 8 should appear in the same location where an external USB drives usually appear. For Windows users, this is typically under "This PC/Computer" menu.

6. Open your device drive to see the different folders present. Note that you may not be able to access the folders if your phone is locked.

7. To transfer files from your PC to your phone. Locate the file you want to transfer on your PC. Then click, drag and drop the file into the corresponding folder on your Phone. For example, image should be dragged to Photos/Gallery folder. Alternatively, if you are using PC, right-click on the file you

want to send, select **Send to** and then choose your phone from the options that appear.
8. Disconnect your phone just as you would disconnect an external memory drive. If you are using Windows 10, you may just remove the USB from the phone when you are done with the transfer. You don't need to click any disconnect icon before you remove your phone if you are using Windows 10.

Note: After the transfer, your transferred files should appear under the corresponding content library on your device. To view any of the transferred files:
From the Home screen, swipe up and tap **Samsung folder > My Files**. Then tap an appropriate category to view the transferred files or folders.
Note that your phone will only recognize the file you transferred if the file it is a supported file type.
If you do factory reset to your phone, you may need to re-transfer the files again (unless you have them stored on a cloud storage like Dropbox).

Wi-Fi

Using your phone, you can connect to the internet or other network devices anywhere an access point or wireless hotspot is available.
To activate the Wi-Fi feature and connect to a network:
1. Swipe down from the top of the screen.

2. Tap and hold the **Wi-Fi** 📶 icon.
3. Tap the switch next to Wi-Fi to turn it on.
4. Your device then automatically scans for available networks and displays them.
5. Select a network and enter a password for the network (if necessary). You may also manually add a network. To manually add a network, scroll down (if necessary) and tap **Add network**. Then follow the on-screen instructions.
6. To turn Wi-Fi off, swipe down from the top of the screen and tap **Wi-Fi** 📶.

Notes:

- The Wi-Fi feature running in the background will consume battery. To save battery, put it off whenever you are not using it.
- The Wi-Fi may not connect a network if the network signal is not very good.
- When Wi-Fi is connected, active, and communicating with a wireless Access Point, **Wi-Fi active** is displayed in the Status bar.

Using Your Phone as a Hotspot

If your network provider supports it, you can use this feature to share your mobile network with friends.

1. Swipe down from the top of the screen and select the settings icon ⚙. Tap **Connections** tab.
2. Tap **Mobile hotspot and tethering**.
3. Tap **Mobile hotspot**.
4. Next to Mobile Hotspot, tap **On**. Please note that Wi-Fi will need to be turned off for you to turn on mobile hotspot.
5. To set the password and enable password protection, tap the menu icon ⋮ (located at the top of the screen) and tap **Configure Mobile Hotspot**. Enter a name for the network (this is the name that other devices searching for the network will see). Scroll down and tap **Password**. Then enter a password for the network and tap **Save**.

6. After enabling the mobile hotspot, your friends should be able to connect to it just like they connect to wireless networks.

Hints:

You can choose who connect to your mobile hotspot by creating the Allowed Device list. To do this:

1. Follow steps 1 to 4 above.

2. Tap the menu icon ⋮ > **Allowed devices**, and then tap **Add** to enter the device name and MAC address. The MAC address of many smart gadgets is found under **Wi-Fi settings** or **Wi-Fi Advanced settings.**

4. Tap **Add** to add the device.

5. Tap the status switch next to **Allowed devices only** to make sure only the allowed devices can connect to your mobile hotspot.

6. To delete an allowed device, tap and hold the device and select **DELETE.**

In addition, you can automatically turn off Mobile hotspot if there are no connected devices. To do this, follow the step 1 above. Then tap the menu icon ⋮ > **Timeout settings**, and then select a time.

Access More by Using Bluetooth

Bluetooth option allows you to connect to another Bluetooth device within range.

Note: If there are obstacles, the operating distance of the Bluetooth may be reduced. The Bluetooth communication range is usually approximately 30 feet.

To use Bluetooth feature:
1. Swipe down from the top of the screen.

2. Tap and hold the **Bluetooth** icon .
3. Then next to **Bluetooth**, select **on.**
4. Then Bluetooth automatically scans for nearby Bluetooth devices and displays them. Please make sure the Bluetooth of the device you are connecting with is turned on and discoverable.
5. Tap a device to connect with and follow the prompts to finish the connection. You may need to enter a pairing code.
6. When connected, the **Bluetooth icon** will appear next to the **Wi-Fi icon** on the Status bar. Pairing between two Bluetooth devices is a one-time process. Once two devices are paired, the devices continue to recognize this association and you may not need to re-enter a passcode.
7. To turn Bluetooth off, swipe down from the top of the screen, tap **Bluetooth** . The Bluetooth will appear gray when you turn it off.

Unpairing a Paired Device

1. Swipe down from the top of the screen.
2. Tap and hold the **Bluetooth** icon.
3. Then next to **Bluetooth**, select **on** (if not already turned on).
4. Tap the settings icon next to the paired device, and then tap **Unpair** to delete the paired device.

Tip: Once you have paired your device to another device, you can rename the paired device to make it easier to recognize. To do this, follow the steps 1 to 3 above and tap the settings icon ⚙ next to the previously paired device. Then tap **Rename**. Enter a new name, and tap **Rename**.

Location Services

Enabling location service allows apps to serve you content related services.

Note: You may have to activate location service to receive information and search the map.

To activate location services:
1. Swipe down from the top of the screen and select the settings icon ⚙. Tap **Connection**.
2. Tap **Location**.
3. Next to the switch under **Location**, select **on**.
4. To put it off, tap the switch again.

Tip: If you want your phone to use a combination of Wi-Fi, GPS, and mobile networks to estimate your location, tap **Location Method** and then tap **High accuracy**.

Find My Mobile Feature

You can use this feature to locate your phone if lost.

Note: You must sign up for a Samsung account and enable location service (as explained above) to use **Find My Mobile**.

To add Samsung account (if you have not done so before):

1. Swipe down from the top of the screen and select the settings icon ✪.

2. Tap **Cloud and accounts**.

3. Tap **Account**.

4. Tap **Add account**.

5. Tap **Samsung Account**. Then enter your Samsung account information.

6. Or tap **CREATE ACCOUNT** and follow the prompts.
   Please note that if you have already added Samsung account, you can skip these steps.

To activate Find My Mobile Feature:

1. Swipe down from the top of the screen and select the settings icon ✪.

2. Tap **Lock screen and security**.

3. Tap **Find My Mobile**.

4. If required, enter your Samsung account's password and then tap **Sign In.** If you don't have a Samsung account, create one.

5. Make sure that the status switches beside **Remote Controls**, **Google Location Service** and **Send Last Location** are turned on.

To find your lost phone:

1. Open a web browser **findmymobile.samsung.com**
2. Tap **Sign In.**

3. Enter the email address associated with your Samsung account into the email field and then enter your password. Click **Sign In.**

4. If you have more than one phone, you may need to select your Samsung Galaxy Note 8 (if it is not currently displayed). To do this, tap the dropdown arrow next to the current device name and select your device name.

5. Tap **FIND**.

6. Tap the dropdown menu icon to access the map.

The current location of your phone will be displayed on a map. You can use the options on this website to **ring your device, lock your device, back up your device, and wipe your device**.

Tip: You can use **Find My Device** to unlock your device when you forget your log in information. To do this, follow the steps 1-5 above and tap **MORE**. Then select **UNLOCK MY DEVICE** and enter your Samsung account password.

Note: Please note that your phone may need to be connected to a wireless or mobile network to be able to use the **Find My Mobile** feature to manage your phone. However, you may still be able to know the last known location of your phone.

Using the NFC (Near Field Communication)

This is a technology similar to Bluetooth and Wi-Fi. It utilizes electromagnetic radio frequency. Devices using NFC may be passive or active. A passive device is not powered by battery but contains information that other devices can read but does not read any information itself. An example of a passive NFC is NFC tag. On the other hand, an active NFC device can read information and send it. An example of an active NFC device is your Samsung Galaxy Note 8.

You can use NFC feature to send files from your phone to other NFC supported devices.

To turn on and use NFC:
1. Swipe down from the top of the screen using two fingers then tap and hold the **NFC** icon for two or three seconds. Please note that you may need to swipe to the right to access more quick settings options before you can see the **NFC** icon.
2. Under **NFC and payment,** tap the switch to turn it on. Also make sure the status switch next to **Android Beam** is turned on.

Note: To use NFC to send a file to another device, ensure both devices involved have their NFC turned on. Then open the file you wish to send and tap **Share**. Tap **Android Beam**. Hold your mobile phone and the receiving device back to back. Then tap the screen to send the file.

It may not be very effective in sending large files because it may be slow.

Using NFC to make payment

In recent times, NFC is finding more usage in payment system.

Making payments with the NFC feature:

1. Follow steps 1 and 2 above (under **To turn on and use NFC)**.
2. Touch the back of your device to the NFC card reader

Usually, after you have enabled NFC payments on your phone, you should be able to make payments for items by tapping your phone against a participating store's NFC reader.

You can also select the default payment application you want to use for making purchases on your device. To do this, when on the **NFC and payment** screen, tap **Tap and pay** and then tap **PAYMENT**. Then select a default payment app.

Settings

Settings menu give you the opportunity to customize your device as you like.

To access the settings menu
1. Swipe down from the top of the screen and select the settings icon ⚙.
2. Alternatively, swipe up from the Home screen and then tap **Settings**.
3. Tap a setting category.

Search for Settings

It is advisable to use the searching feature when you are not sure exactly where to find a certain setting.
1. Swipe down from the top of the screen and select the settings icon ⚙.
2. Tap **Search icon** (the lens icon located at the top of the screen).
3. Enter a word or words in the Search field. The list filters as you write.
4. Tap an option (make sure you select the best match).

Hint: There is a tip to getting what you want from your device. From time to time, you will want to customize your phone in a special way. All you need to do in a period like this is to open the settings as described above. Then tap the search tab and enter a search word or phrase.

What You Must Know About Samsung Galaxy Note 8

How to Find Your Phone When lost

As a human being, it is not impossible that you may misplace your phone. If someone else (a thief) has not taken custody of it, there are steps to follow to find it. These steps have been discussed at length in the previous chapter; please refer page 305 for details.

How to Reduce Your Mobile Data Usage on Samsung Galaxy Note 8

If you realize that you are using more MB/Data than normal, there are steps to follow to reduce your data consumption.

1. The first thing is to make sure that you update apps on Wi-Fi only. To do this:

    a. Swipe up from the Home screen and tap **Play Store**.

    b. Tap the menu icon.

    c. Tap **Settings**.

d. Tap **Auto-update apps** and select **Auto-update apps over Wi-Fi only.**

2. Consider using a data friendly browser: Browser like **Opera Mini** gives you the opportunity to save data through their **data saving** feature. You can also control the picture quality of webpages when you are using Opera Mini browser and thereby saving data. To download Opera Mini, please visit Google Play store.

3. Enable Data saver: To do this, from a Home screen, tap the **settings icon** ⚙. Tap **Connections**. Tap **Data usage** and then tap **Data saver**. Tap the status switch next to **Data saver**.

To control the number of apps that have unrestricted access to your data, tap **Allow app while Data saver on.**

Solution to Non-Responding Apps

Sometimes an app may start misbehaving and may even refuse to close. The first thing you can do in a situation like this is to tap on the recent button . This gives you an access to all opened/running apps on your phone. Locate this app, and tap **X** icon to close it. Try launching the app again.

If it is still misbehaving after closing it or it refuses to close, then you may try these steps:

1. Swipe down from the top of the screen and select the settings icon .
2. Tap **Apps**.
3. Then tap on the misbehaving application from the list of applications.
4. Select **FORCE STOP**. This will stop the app from carrying out any process on your phone. To enable the app again, just launch the app.

Note: Please restart your device if stopping an app causes your device to stop working correctly.

How to Conserve Samsung Galaxy Note 8's Battery Life

You may notice that you have to charge Samsung Galaxy Note 8 twice a day to keep it on. There are steps to follow to ensure that your phone serves you throughout the day with just a single charge.

1. **Reduce the screen brightness and turn off the automatic brightness:** I have realized over time that screen brightness consumes a lot of energy. There is usually a substantial difference between using a phone with a maximum brightness and using it with a moderate brightness. As a rule, don't use your phone with a maximum brightness unless you can't see what is on the screen clearly. For example, if you are outdoor. Make sure you reduce it immediately when it is no more needed.
2. **Shorten the Screen timeout:** if you really want to save your battery life, you must try to shorten the screen timeout. Reducing how long your phone will stay lit up after you finish interacting with it will really help you to save your battery. To manage screen timeout setting:
    a. Swipe down from the top of the screen and select the settings icon ⚙ .
    b. Tap **Display**.
    c. Scroll down and tap on **Screen Timeout**. Then choose an option.

[Screenshot of SCREEN TIMEOUT settings with options: 15 seconds, 30 seconds (selected), 1 minute, 2 minutes, 5 minutes, 10 minutes. An arrow points to "1 minute" labeled "Choose an option".]

3. **Turn off Wi-Fi and Bluetooth:** when you are not using Wi-Fi or Bluetooth, please always remember to put them off. These features really consume energy and they are better off when not in use.

4. **Reduce number of notifications:** there are two benefits of doing this. The first is that there will be less distractions and the second benefit is that notification consumes energy. Limit yourself to those notifications that are important to your life. To manage notification setting for an app:

    a. Swipe down from the top of the screen and select the settings icon ⚙ .

    b. Tap **Apps**.

    c. Tap an app.

d. Tap on **Notifications** to configure the notifications setting for the chosen app.
5. **Close all unnecessary apps:** the truth is that any app you are accessing is consuming out of the limited battery energy. It is important to close any app you are not using from time to time. To access all apps currently running on your phone, tap on the recent button ⟳ and then tap **X** icon next to the application you want to close.
6. **Use a correct charger:** using a wrong charger can endanger the health of your phone/battery, and it is better to avoid such practice.
7. **Consider switching off your phone:** if you are not going to use your phone for an extended period, you may consider switching off your phone.
8. **Use headphones:** using the headphones is another cool way to save your battery. Extended use of audio speakers of your phone may drain your battery faster.

What to Do if You Forget You Device Lock Screen Password/Pin

1. Open a web browser **findmymobile.samsung.com**
2. Tap **Sign In**.

3. Enter the email address associated with your Samsung account into the email field and then enter your password. Click **Sign In**.

4. If you have more than one phone, you may need to select your Samsung Galaxy Note 8 (if it is not currently displayed). To do this, click the dropdown arrow next to the current device name and select your device name.

5. Tap **FIND**.

6. Tap **MORE**. Then select **UNLOCK MY DEVICE** and enter your Samsung account information.

Please note that if you have disabled **Remote Controls**, you will need to activate it before you can use the method above. To do this:

1. Swipe down from the top of the screen and select the settings icon ⚙.
2. Tap **Lock screen and security**.
3. Tap **Find My Mobile**.
4. Enter your Samsung account information and then tap **Sign In**. If you don't have a Samsung account, then create one.
5. Make sure that the status switches beside **Remote Controls**, **Google Location Service** and **Send Last Location** are turned on.

322

How to Take Screenshot on Your Device

Another task you can perform on your device is taking a screenshot. Capturing a screenshot should automatically create a Screenshot folder.

To take a screenshot with your device, please follow the instructions below:

Method 1

Press and hold the volume down key and the power key simultaneously until you hear a small sound. You can view captured images in Gallery.

Method 2

You can also capture screenshots by swiping your hand to the left or right across the screen. To be able to use this method, you have to enable it. To do this:

1. Swipe down from the top of the screen and select the settings icon ⚙.

2. Scroll down and tap **Advanced features**.

3. Tap **Palm swipe to capture** and then tap the status switch to activate it.

To capture a screenshot when this feature is enabled, just swipe the edge of your hand across more than half of the screen.

The Smart capture

You can capture a screen and the scrollable area. In addition, you can immediately crop and share the captured screen. This feature is usually enabled by default, but if you want to check whether it is enabled or not, please follow the instructions below:

1. Swipe down from the top of the screen and select the settings icon ⚙.

2. Scroll down and tap **Advanced features**.
3. Tap **Smart capture**, and then tap the status switch to activate it.

Thereafter, press and hold the volume down key and the power key simultaneously to take a screenshot. Then tap on any of these options:

| Bixby Vision | Scroll capture | Draw | Crop | Share |

Bixby Vision: Tap this icon to get more information about the screenshot you have captured. To learn more about Bixby Vision, please go to page 202.

Scroll Capture: Use this to capture the hidden parts of the screen. When you tap this icon, the screen will automatically scroll down, and more content will be captured. To capture more screen, tap this icon again.

Draw: Use this option to annotate the screenshot.

Crop: Use this to crop a portion from the screenshot.

Share: Use this to share the screenshot.

Extras

What You Must Know Before Selling or Giving Away Your Samsung Galaxy Note 8

A time will probably come when you will need to give away or sell your Samsung Galaxy Note 8. There are few things you must know before this time comes.

Some time ago, BBC reported that Avast (an antivirus giant) was able to use publicly available forensic security tools to extracts naked selfies from second-hand phones bought on eBay. Other extracted data were emails, text messages and Google searches.

It is usual for many users to perform factory resets before selling their phones. The truth is that with the advent of sophisticated software, factory reset is no more enough. In fact, you have to go a step further.

So, what can you do to save your privacy? The simple answer is to go a step further by always encrypting your files. You should encrypt all your data before performing factory reset when you are considering selling or giving away your Phone.

However, you must know that encrypting your device before doing the factory reset may not give 100% protection to your privacy. Who knows if programmers will develop a software that will be a step ahead of that in the nearest future? The best way to completely protect your privacy is to destroy your phone when you don't need it again. But as you know, this is not feasible all the time and may not be advisable.

Finally, encrypting your phone before performing factory reset is an efficient way of protecting your privacy. At least it makes it much more difficult for people to retrieve your files.

Interestingly, Samsung Galaxy Note 8 automatically encrypts data stored on it. However, you will need to encrypt data stored on memory card yourself. To do that:

- From the Home screen, swipe up from the bottom of the screen and tap **Settings**.
- Tap **Lock screen and security > Encrypt SD card**.
- Read the onscreen information and if you are satisfied with the information, tap **Encrypt SD card**.

When you encrypt your memory card, you may need a numeric PIN or password to decrypt your SD card when you first access it after switching on your device.

Getting an antivirus for your phone -- is it necessary?

Many people may not really take the issue of antivirus seriously because they think that virus software target PC much more that phones. The truth is that things are changing every now and then. The best thing you can do is to always keep a guard. There are many reputable free antiviruses on Google play store. My favorite antiviruses are AVG, Lookout and Norton Antiviruses. You may check Google Play Store to download any of these.

Note: The best way to protect yourself from a virus attack is being proactive. For example, I don't expect you to click the links present in an unsolicited email. So, having many antiviruses on your phone may not help if you are not prudent in your actions.

Safety Precautions When Using Samsung Galaxy Note 8 on Wi-Fi

With many free Wi-Fi hotspot, it is likely that you are going to find yourself using Wi-Fi more on your phone. There are few things to keep in mind when using Wi-Fi.

1. **Confirm the Network Name**

Hackers sometimes set up a fake Wi-Fi network in order to tap into the information of unwitting public users. To avoid this, make sure you are sure of the name of the network you are connecting to. You may ask any trusted individual around you if you doubt the name of a network.

2. **Connect to a Secured Site**

Whenever you are sending a sensitive information, always make sure that the site is a secured website. You can know whether a website is a secured site or not by checking whether the *url* address of the website starts with **HTTPS.** If it starts with https, then it should be a secured site.

3. **Run an Antivirus Software**

As earlier mentioned, using an antivirus is very crucial in today's world. You may consider installing a genuine antivirus. There are many of them on Google Play store.

4. **Get a Virtual Private Network (VPN)**

It is highly important you use a virtual private network when using a public wireless network. There are both free and paid VPN providers. My favorite is **Hotspot Shield VPN.** It is available on Google Play store. They offer both free and paid versions. You may also check out other VPN apps to pick the best.

5. **Avoid Automatic Connection**

Make sure your Wi-Fi is off when not using it to avoid your phone automatically connecting to an open network. Turning your Wi-Fi off when not using it will also save your battery.

I am Having a Dwindling Love for my Samsung Galaxy Note 8; What Should I Do?

It is possible that after buying Samsung Galaxy Note 8, you realize that it performs below your expectation. It is likely that you dislike your phone because of its hardware or software issue. Generally, the hardware has to do with the design, the phone make up, the weight of the phone etc. While the software has to do with the OS and applications.

If your love for Samsung Galaxy Note 8 is reducing because of the software, there is a way out. You can take your time to look for beneficial apps to install on your device.

If your love for Samsung Galaxy Note 8 is reducing because of the hardware, then it is either you learn how to live with it (you may have to force yourself to love it), give it away or you sell it. If you are considering selling your phone or giving it away, then make sure you read the article on page 326.

TROUBLESHOOTING

If the touch screen responds slowly or improperly or your phone is not responding, try the following:

- Remove any protective covers (screen protector) from the touch screen.
- Ensure that your hands are clean and dry when tapping. In addition, ensure that the screen of your phone is not wet. If wet, use a soft dry towel to dry it.
- Press the power button once to lock the screen and press it again to unlock the screen and enter a PIN/password/pattern if required.
- Switch off your device and on it again.

Your Phone Doesn't Charge

- Make sure you are using Samsung charger to charge your phone.
- If the Samsung Galaxy Note 8 does not indicate that it is charging, unplug the power adapter and then restart your device.
- Make sure you are using the USB cable that came with the Samsung Galaxy Note 8 or anyone that has similar specs.

Your device is hot to the touch

When you use applications that require more power or use applications on your device for an extended period, your phone may be a bit hot to touch. This is normal, and it should not affect its performance. You may just allow your phone to rest for some time or close some applications.

Your phone freezes or has fatal error

If your phone freezes or it is unresponsive, press and hold the Power key and the Volume Down key simultaneously for more than 7 seconds to restart it.

Phone does not connect to Wi-Fi

Make sure you don't have limited network connectivity in that area. If your network signal is good and you still cannot connect, you may perform any of these actions.

- Make sure your Airplane Mode is off.
- Try restarting the Wi-Fi.
- Move closer to your router and scan for the available networks. If the network still does not show up, you may add the network manually.
- Restart your router and modem. Unplug the modem and router for few minutes and plug the modem in, and then the router.
- Try restarting you phone.

Phone screen color is appearing somehow

- Check if you have not mistakenly turned on blue light filter.

  To do this, go to **Settings** ⚙ **> Display > Blue Light Filter > Turn on now**.

Another Bluetooth device is not located

- Ensure Bluetooth feature is activated on your phone and the device you want to connect to.
- Ensure that your phone and the other Bluetooth device are within the maximum Bluetooth range (usually approximately 30 feet).

A connection is not established when you connect your phone to a PC

- Ensure that the USB cable you are using is compatible with your device.
- Ensure that you have the proper drivers installed and updated on your PC.

Audio quality is poor during a call

- Ensure that the network signal is strong. When you are in an area with a weak or poor reception, you may lose reception. Try moving to another area and then try again.

Safety precautions

A. To prevent electric shock, fire, and explosion
1. Do not use damaged power cords or plugs, or loose electrical sockets.
2. Do not touch the power cord with a wet hand.
3. Do not bend or damage the power cord.
4. Do not short-circuit the charger.
5. Do not use your phone during thunderstorm.
6. Do not dispose your phone by putting it in fire.

B. Follow all safety warnings and regulations when using your device in restricted areas.
C. Comply with all safety warnings and regulations regarding mobile device usage while operating a vehicle.
D. Proper care and use of your phone
1. Do not use or store your phone in hot or cold areas. It is recommended to use your device at temperature from 5^0C to 35^0C.
2. Do not put your phone near magnetic fields.
3. Do not use camera flash close to eyes of people or pets because it can cause temporary loss of vision or damage the eyes.
4. When speaking on the phone, speak directly into the mouthpiece.
5. Avoid disturbing others when using your phone in public.

6. Keep your phone away from small children because they may mistakenly damage it as it may look like a toy to them.

Just Before You Go (Please Read!)

Although I have put in tremendous effort into writing this guide, I am confident that I have not said it all.

I have no doubt believing that I have not written everything possible about this device.

So, I want you to do me a favor.

If you will like to know how to perform a task that is not included in this guide, please let me know by sending me an email at **pharmibrahimguides@gmail.com**. I will try as much as possible to reply you as soon as I can.

You may also visit my author's page at

www.amazon.com/author/pharmibrahim

And please don't forget to follow me when you visit my author's page, just click or tap on **Follow** button located below the profile picture.

Printed in Great Britain
by Amazon